Science, Grade 4

Table of Contents

Unit 3: Life Science

Introduction

Children see the world around them and ask questions that naturally lead into the lessons that they will be taught in science. Science is exciting to children because it answers their questions about themselves and the world around them—their immediate world and their larger environment. They should be encouraged to observe their world, the things in it, and how things interact. A basic understanding of science boosts students' understanding of the world around them.

Organization

Science provides information on a variety of basic science concepts. It is broken into three units: Physical Science, Earth and Space Science, and Life Science. Each unit contains concise background information on the unit's topics, as well as exercises and activities to reinforce students' knowledge and understanding of basic principles of science and the world around them.

This book contains three types of pages:

- Concise background information is provided for each unit. These pages are intended for the teacher's use or for helpers to read to the class.

- Assessments are included for use as tests or practice for the students. These pages are meant to be reproduced.

- Activity pages contain information on a subject, or they list the materials and steps necessary for students to complete a project. Questions for students to answer are also included on these pages as a type of performance assessment. As much as possible, these activities include most of the multiple intelligences so students can use their strengths to achieve a well-balanced learning style. These pages are also meant for reproduction for use by students.

Use

Science is designed for independent use by students who have been introduced to the skills and concepts described. Copies of the activities can be given to individuals, pairs of students, or small groups for completion. They may also be used as a center activity. If students are familiar with the content, the worksheets may also be used as homework.

Hands-On Experience

An understanding of science is best promoted by hands-on experience. *Science* provides a wide variety of activities for students to do. But students also need real-life exposure to their world. Playgrounds, parks, and vacant lots are handy study sites to observe many of nature's forces and changes.

It is essential that students be given sufficient concrete examples of scientific concepts. Appropriate manipulatives can be bought or made from common everyday objects. Most of the activity pages can be completed with materials easily accessible to the students.

Suggestions for Use

- **Bulletin Board:** Display completed work to show student progress.

- **Portfolios:** Have your students maintain a portfolio of their completed exercises and activities or of newspaper articles about current events in science. This portfolio can help you in performance assessment.

- **Assessments:** Use the overall and unit assessments as diagnostic tools by administering them before students begin the activities. After students have completed each unit, let them retake the unit test to see the progress they have made.

- **Center Activities:** Use the worksheets as a center activity to give students the opportunity to work cooperatively.

- **Fun:** Have fun with these activities while you and your students uncover the basic principles of science.

FOSS Correlation

The Full Option Science System™ (FOSS) was developed at the University of California at Berkeley. It is a coordinated science curriculum organized into four categories: Life Science; Physical Science; Earth Science; and Scientific Reasoning and Technology. Under each category are various modules that span two grade levels. The modules for this grade level are highlighted in the chart below.

Physical Science
- Magnetism & Electricity: See *Science*, grade 3, and *Science*, grade 5, in this series.
- Physics of Sound: 32–43

Earth Science
- Earth Materials: 71–88
- Water: 89, 95, 96, 98, 100–102

Life Science
- Human Body: 159–170
- Structures of Life: 125–147

Overall Assessment

☐ **Read each statement. Write *T* on the line if the statement is true. Write *F* if the statement is false.**

_____ **1.** A doorknob is the wheel part of a wheel and axle.

_____ **2.** Smooth surfaces cause more friction than rough surfaces.

_____ **3.** Sound is a form of energy.

_____ **4.** Sound waves hit the eardrum inside the ear to make it vibrate.

_____ **5.** Light sources are objects that make light.

_____ **6.** Light travels very slowly.

☐ **Darken the letter of the answer that best completes each sentence.**

7. Wedges are used to _____.
- Ⓐ stick things together
- Ⓑ break things apart
- Ⓒ lift things
- Ⓓ lower things

8. There is friction whenever _____.
- Ⓐ two surfaces rub together
- Ⓑ an object does not move
- Ⓒ an object is weighed
- Ⓓ an object is lifted

9. Sound is made when an object _____.
- Ⓐ breaks
- Ⓑ vibrates
- Ⓒ cools
- Ⓓ stops

10. Sound travels in _____.
- Ⓐ zigzags
- Ⓑ particles
- Ⓒ waves
- Ⓓ lines

11. _____ makes its own light.
- Ⓐ The Moon
- Ⓑ A firefly
- Ⓒ The Earth
- Ⓓ Mars

12. When all the colors of the spectrum are reflected, an object will look _____.
- Ⓐ blue
- Ⓑ red
- Ⓒ black
- Ⓓ white

GO ON TO THE NEXT PAGE ☞

Overall Assessment, p. 2

☐ Read each statement. Write *T* on the line if the statement is true. Write *F* if the statement is false.

_____ **13.** The top layer of the Earth is called the crust.

_____ **14.** Rocks cannot be broken apart.

_____ **15.** The Sun is the Earth's main source of heat and light.

_____ **16.** The Moon gives off its own light.

_____ **17.** A fault is a crack in the Earth's crust.

_____ **18.** A thermometer is used to measure air pressure.

☐ Darken the letter of the answer that best completes each sentence.

19. The layer of the Earth that is the hottest is the _____.
Ⓐ core
Ⓑ mantle
Ⓒ crust
Ⓓ surface

20. An earthquake is _____.
Ⓐ an opening in the Earth's crust through which lava escapes
Ⓑ a sudden movement in the Earth's crust
Ⓒ never the cause of much damage
Ⓓ a kind of chemical weathering

21. The two main gases in the Earth's atmosphere are nitrogen and _____.
Ⓐ oxygen
Ⓑ water vapor
Ⓒ carbon dioxide
Ⓓ hydrogen

22. The water cycle is _____.
Ⓐ the movement of water between the air and the ground
Ⓑ a form of transportation
Ⓒ a weather symbol
Ⓓ an air mass

23. Clouds, rain, air temperature, and wind are all part of the Earth's _____.
Ⓐ core
Ⓑ plates
Ⓒ ionosphere
Ⓓ weather

24. The entire lighted surface of the Moon faces the Earth _____.
Ⓐ when the Moon is full
Ⓑ during a lunar eclipse
Ⓒ when the Moon is new
Ⓓ during a solar eclipse

GO ON TO THE NEXT PAGE ☞

Overall Assessment, p. 3

Read each statement. Write *T* on the line if the statement is true. Write *F* if the statement is false.

_____ **25.** Living things do not need food or water.

_____ **26.** Life on Earth is contained in the biosphere.

_____ **27.** All populations of living things are exactly alike.

_____ **28.** Decomposers make food for consumers to eat.

_____ **29.** You only need to brush your teeth when you eat candy.

_____ **30.** Poison ivy can cause a rash.

Darken the letter of the answer that best completes each sentence.

31. A community is made up of several _____.
Ⓐ foods
Ⓑ populations
Ⓒ oil spills
Ⓓ muscles

32. A food web is made up of several _____.
Ⓐ spiders
Ⓑ restaurants
Ⓒ food chains
Ⓓ decomposers

33. Plants make their own food through the process of _____.
Ⓐ cooking
Ⓑ condensation
Ⓒ photography
Ⓓ photosynthesis

34. Smoke is a form of air _____.
Ⓐ pollution
Ⓑ pressure
Ⓒ conditioning
Ⓓ evaporation

35. People who eat a balanced diet get enough _____, vitamins, and minerals.
Ⓐ bacon
Ⓑ nutrients
Ⓒ soda
Ⓓ exercise

36. A small cut should be washed with _____.
Ⓐ milk
Ⓑ ink
Ⓒ soap and water
Ⓓ alcohol

Unit 1: Physical Science

BACKGROUND INFORMATION

Force

A force is simply a push or a pull. Forces can be balanced or unbalanced, and the interactions of these forces create motion. If forces are balanced, there is no movement. Forces also differ in size and direction. Forces can come from up, down, left, and right.

Force is measured in newtons. Forces can be added and subtracted. If forces are going in the same direction, they are added. For example, if someone is pushing a wagon and another person is pulling the wagon, the amount of force being exerted can be added together. However, if people are pulling in opposite directions, as in a tug-of-war, the forces would be subtracted. The team having the greater number of newtons would have a greater force and would win.

Motion

The motion of an object is the result when a variety of forces interact. A change in motion occurs if a still object moves, or an object already in motion changes speed or direction. Two different forces, acting in opposite directions, will interact so an object will not move. These forces are considered balanced forces. An unbalanced force results when a force is placed on an object either at rest or in motion, making the object change its state. The object will move faster as the forces become more unbalanced. The greater the imbalance, the faster and farther the object will move.

Friction

Friction is a force that keeps resting objects from moving and tends to slow motion when one object rubs against another object. Every motion is affected by friction. An object's surface determines the amount of friction. Rough surfaces create more friction. Smooth surfaces have less friction, so motion is easier. Mass and surface areas of objects also affect the amount of friction. The heavier an object is, the greater the

amount of friction. Similarly, when large surface areas come into contact during motion, friction is greater. By reducing the contact of the surface areas, such as with wheels, the object can be moved more easily. In some cases, friction can be reduced by using lubricants, materials like oil or soap. Lubricants coat the surface of an object to decrease rubbing.

Machines

Machines are devices that help make work easier. They usually change the amount or direction of forces needed to get a job done by lifting, pulling, pushing, or carrying. A simple machine has no moving parts or only a few moving parts. There are six kinds of simple machines: levers, inclined planes, wedges, screws, pulleys, and wheels and axles. When one or more of these are joined in one machine, it is a compound machine. The end result is that less force is needed to do work.

Levers

A lever is a bar or board that rests on a point, called a fulcrum. If you push down on one end of the bar, the other end rises. The direction of the force is changed. By using a lever, heavy objects can be lifted because less force is needed. Most levers place the fulcrum in the center. The load and the force are at each end. This is known as a first-class lever. When levers are used to lift loads, the force is always applied down. The closer the fulcrum is to the load, the easier the work is, generally.

Inclined Planes

An inclined plane is a flat surface that slopes. Even though the distance to move an object is greater, less work is required to move an object up an inclined plane than to lift it. A ramp is the most common kind of inclined plane. The angle of the plane also affects the force needed to move an object up a ramp. The steeper the plane, the more force is needed to move an object.

Wedges

A wedge is a kind of inclined plane. It is made when two inclined planes are joined together to form one sharp edge. Wedges are often used to break something into two parts. The force is applied at the point, giving a greater force to make the work easier. A thinner wedge will not need as much force as one that is larger. Axes, forks, knives, and needles are examples of wedges.

Screws

A screw is an inclined plane that wraps around a rod to make a spiral. The edge or ridge of the screw is known as the thread. The thread moves between the wood to break it apart as the screw is turned. Like other inclined planes, screws decrease the amount of force needed to work but increase the distance needed to move. Screws often are used to fasten things together, make holes, or lift objects. Other examples of screws are the stem of a car jack, power drills, pencil sharpeners, and spiral staircases.

Pulleys

A pulley is a wheel with a rope wrapped around it. The wheel generally has a groove in it to keep the rope from slipping off. It is also a kind of lever used to lift heavy things. One end of the rope is tied to the object and the other end is pulled by a person or machine. The wheel turns freely, so there is little friction with the rope. There are two kinds of pulleys, fixed and movable. A fixed pulley stays in place as the load is lifted. When someone pulls on the end of the rope, the direction of the force is changed. In movable pulleys, the pulley is attached to the load, leaving it free to move with the load. A movable pulley is lifted.

Wheels and Axles

A wheel and axle is another kind of lever. It uses a handle to turn around the rod, a fulcrum. When the wheel turns, the rod turns; and when the rod turns, the wheel turns. The axle usually goes through the center of the rod. By turning the axle, speed and distance are increased, but more force is needed. By turning the wheel, more force is gained, but the speed and distance are decreased. Examples of axles and wheels include door knobs, screwdrivers, fishing reels, and pencil sharpeners.

Gears are often used in a wheel and axle system. The wheels are notched with "teeth." Usually two or more gears work together in a machine. Gears connected by a chain, such as in a bicycle, move in the same direction. Gears in which the teeth dovetail, move in opposite directions. One gear is often bigger than the others. Even though the distance the large gear travels is greater, causing more effort, the speed of the smaller wheel increases. The speed is determined by the number of notches in a gear. The ratio of large to small notches is often proportional. For example, a large gear may have 20 notches, and a smaller gear will have 10 notches. For each time the large gear turns, the smaller will move twice as fast.

Sound

Energy is the use of a force to move an object. Light, heat, and electricity are all forms of energy that cause movement. Sound is another kind of energy that is made from vibrating objects. As an object begins to vibrate, the surrounding molecules also begin to move. Traveling in sound waves, the molecules collide with other objects in their path. The sound energy is transferred to those objects, so they, too, begin to vibrate. When the initial vibration stops, the sound stops. Vibrations can be heard, seen, and felt.

Anything that produces energy can make a sound. The wings of a bee move and create a vibration that produces a buzzing sound. A hammer hits a nail and produces a vibration from the contact. When we speak, air rushes out of the windpipe and collides with the vocal cords, tissues controlled by the muscles of the larynx. This collision causes the vocal cords to vibrate, resulting in sound. These sounds become words when the tongue, teeth, and lips shape the sounds.

Sound Waves

Sound waves are invisible. As the molecules move away in all directions, they travel in a concentric pattern. Their motion resembles the pattern made when a stone is tossed into water; as the circles move out, they get larger. But the energy diminishes as they grow.

Sound waves also travel through all matter, although at varying speeds. The only place sound energy cannot travel is in a vacuum. Most sounds we hear travel through air molecules, a gas. Since gas molecules are loosely packed, sound waves generally travel more slowly through air. The standard rate is 332 meters per second. However, the speed of travel increases with higher temperatures, because the gas molecules are moving faster and colliding at an increased rate. When sound travels through water, it averages a speed of 1,433 meters per second. Again, the hotter the liquid, the faster the sound wave travels. Sound waves travel faster through solids. In steel, they can travel 4,999 meters per second.

Loudness

Loudness is measured by the amplitude of a sound wave. Shorter amplitudes have a softer sound. Taller amplitudes have a louder sound. The faster and harder an object vibrates, the greater the amplitude of a wave will be, making the sound louder. High-pitched and low-pitched sounds can be soft or loud. Loudness is measured in units known as decibels. A soft sound, such as breathing, has a decibel reading of 0; it is barely audible. A jet plane's engine has a reading of 160 decibels, a level that is painful to human ears. Any sound that has a reading of more than 130 decibels is dangerous to human ears. Continuous exposure to sounds having high decibels can result in the loss of hearing.

Hearing

The ears help decode the vibrations so that we can hear. The ear is divided into three parts: the outer ear, middle ear, and inner ear. The outside of the ear acts like an inverted megaphone to catch sound waves moving in the air. As the sound waves hit the ear shell, they are reflected inward. The waves move into the auditory canal. The energy of the vibrations is transferred to the air inside the auditory canal. The vibrations hit the tightly stretched tissue of the eardrum, the beginning of the middle ear. It

begins to vibrate, passing the energy to three small bones in the ear. The bones increase the vibrations. From there, the vibrations pass to the inner ear. In the inner ear, the vibrations transfer the energy to the liquid-filled cochlea. As the liquid picks up the vibrations, it moves tiny hairs. The hairs change the vibrations into electric signals. The electric signals travel through the auditory nerve to the brain. The brain then decodes the signals to recognizable sounds we can understand.

Technology

Telephones, videotapes, and CDs are all useful technologies that produce sound. Oceanographers map the ocean floor using sound waves. Devices called echo sounders send sound waves to the ocean floor. They bounce back to be received on a reciprocating machine. Scientists know the speed that sound travels in water, so they calculate the time it takes for the sound wave to return to the ship. Waves that return quickly indicate the ocean floor is at a shorter distance, perhaps an ocean mountain. Those that take longer to return indicate a deeper ocean depth.

Light

Light is another form of energy given off in tiny particles called photons. Photons are not a kind of matter, but they move in waves. Thus, light energy exhibits characteristics of both particles and waves. Like sound waves, light waves can move through all matter. However, whereas sound cannot move through a vacuum, photons can. Photons move quickly, too, more quickly than anything else in nature. They travel at a rate of about 300,000 kilometers per second through air, whereas sound only travels 334 meters per second.

Light can be produced from both natural and artificial sources. Natural light is produced by the Sun, the most important source, stars, and fireflies. Light from a natural source is called white light. Artificial light is the product of electricity and reactions that can be controlled, such as flashlights, light bulbs, fires, and candles. Some objects appear to be a light source, but they simply reflect a natural light source. The Moon is an example of a reflective object. Light from the Sun strikes the Moon. The light bounces back, or reflects, making the Moon look as if it is emitting a light. Because light travels so quickly, the whole process takes about three seconds.

Movement

Light travels in a straight path from its source, moving away in all directions. But the farther a light beam is from its source, the more the beam diffuses. Light near its source is brighter and more intense because the photons are more dense. Conversely, the farther you move away from the light source, the dimmer the light appears. Because light has the tendency to move in a straight line, we cannot see around corners.

When light hits an object, the object blocks the light, causing a shadow to form. A shadow is the dark area behind an object resulting from the blocking of light waves. Shadows are made when the object is in the path of a light beam. Moreover, the closer the object is to the source, the sharper the shadow will be. The farther an object is from the light source, the more the shadow will be blurred around the edges.

The makeup of the object affects the movement of the light beam. Materials are identified as either transparent, translucent, or opaque. A transparent object, like glass and clear plastic, allows the light to move through, much like a sound wave moves through a solid. Light essentially travels in a straight path through a transparent object. Transparent objects are clear and easily seen through. A translucent object is blurry when you look through it. As light travels through a translucent object, it bends slightly. Because the light bends, the material looks blurry. Opaque objects totally block the light. Since light cannot travel through an opaque object, you cannot see through it.

Reflection and Absorption

Most objects do not produce light. We can see them because of the process of reflection and absorption. Reflection occurs when a light beam collides with an object. The beam bounces back, much like a ball thrown against the floor. When the reflected light hits the eye, we can see the object. Absorption is the process in which a light beam, or parts of a light beam, soak into the object. Some objects absorb part of the beam, while the rest of the beam is reflected.

Flat Reflectors

The surface of an object also affects the reaction of light. Some surfaces are shiny and smooth. Light reflects, or bounces off, easily. Mirrors and polished metals are good reflectors. When a light beam collides with a reflective surface, the beam bounces back at a corresponding angle. The incoming beam is the angle of incidence, and it is equal to the angle of reflection, the outgoing beam. If the surface is uneven, the beam reacts differently. The particles scatter in all directions. So even if a surface is shiny, it is not a good reflector if the surface is uneven.

Flat mirrors are the best reflectors. The image seen in a mirror is reversed. Moreover, the distance the object is from the mirror is the distance the image appears behind the mirror. Because of their surface, mirrors can easily change the direction of light. Because light bounces off at the same angle it enters, mirrors have multiple functions. Used in pairs, mirrors help us to see beyond barriers and around corners by bending light.

Curved Reflectors

Some mirrors are curved. Light reflects off a curved mirror much as it would if a series of flat mirrors were set at angles to each other. As the light particles hit each mirror, they bounce in many directions but still at an equal angle to the incoming beam. With mirrors curved inward, the light rays can be reflected to a single spot, called a focal point. Curved mirrors focus light, making the light brighter and more intense. Flashlights, headlights, microscopes, and telescopes use curved mirrors.

Mirrors can curve in or out. Mirrors curved in, like the inside of a spoon, are called concave. The reflection from a concave mirror is larger because the light rays spread out. On the other hand, the outside of a spoon is an example of a convex mirror. It curves out, making an image look smaller. The convex mirror bends light so the rays come together.

Refraction

Light can travel through different materials. The reaction of the light depends on two factors: whether the material is transparent or translucent and what kind of matter the object is. The density of the material affects the speed. A material that is dense will slow the speed of light. When the speed of light changes, it bends. This bending is called refraction. Refraction helps us to see transparent objects. For example, light travels through the air and hits glass. Because the glass is clear, light can move through it. However, since it is a different material, the light slows and bends, allowing us to see the glass when the light bends.

Refraction is also the reason for apparent tricks to the eyes, such as a straw in water which looks like it has been cut. Above water, light hits the straw first. But below water, light hits the water and bends before encountering the straw. The bending makes the straw look as if it is cut in half.

Lenses

Lenses are curved pieces of glass or clear plastic. Like mirrors, lenses can be convex, concave, or flat. Since they have a front and back, they may have a combination of sides, such as a flat front and a concave back. As light moves from the air to the lens, it bends. As the light beam exits the lens, it bends a second time when it enters the air again. Convex lenses are thicker in the middle and, like convex mirrors, bend light to a focal point. The thickness of the glass affects how much the light beam bends. Also, a lens with a sharper curve bends light more sharply. The concave lens is thinner in the middle. It spreads light out.

Many devices utilize lenses. Eyeglasses use both concave or convex lenses to improve eyesight. Microscopes use lenses to make small things look bigger, and telescopes use them so that distant objects seem closer. Cameras also use lenses. The camera lens focuses the light so an image appears on film.

Color

Sir Isaac Newton was the first person to discover that light was actually comprised of a spectrum of seven colors: red, orange, yellow, green, blue, indigo, and violet. The s
stays in the same color order and car
remembered using the name ROY G
color has a different wavelength. Rec
longest wavelength, and violet is the
Since the photons travel at different
they bend at different rates as they p
a transparent object.

A prism is a triangular piece of
commonly used to separate colors. L
light leaves the air and enters the pri
it slows and bends. As it exits the gl
travels into the air, it bends again. Bo
colors move in different wavelengths
travel at different speeds. They bend
degrees, resulting in a separation we

Rainbows are created in a simil
the raindrops act like prisms. Sunligl
the drop, and because of the drop's r
shape, the sunlight reflects back to th
it leaves the drop, it bends again. Th
causes the sunlight to spread out eve
With millions of drops refracting and
sunlight, a rainbow appears.

Seeing Colors

As white light collides with an objec
whole color spectrum also hits the ol
object reflects its color, absorbing all
colors of the white light. In other wo
yellow ball appears yellow because t
wavelength reflects back to our eyes.
colors are absorbed. To appear white
object reflects the entire spectrum. To
black, the black object absorbs all the
When an object is transparent, such a
glass vase, the green light passes thro
instead of being reflected; the other c
absorbed by the glass.

How We See

The eyeball is covered by a cornea, w
protective film covering the eye. The
circle on the eye is the iris. The pupil
circle, is inside the iris. The iris enlar
shrinks the pupil to control the amoun
that enters the inside of the eyeball. T
shrinks in bright light to reduce the ar
light and enlarges when more light is
see. Once light enters the pupil, it mo

ough the lens. The cornea and the lens work ether to bend the light so the reflection uses on the retina in the back of the eye. The age appears on the retina. From there, the ssage moves through the optic nerve to the in. The brain then interprets the message as icture.

When a part of the eye is not working or eyeball changes shape, people may have uble seeing; the image is not being focused the retina. In nearsighted people, people who e difficulty seeing distant objects, the focus n front of the retina. Glasses with concave lenses can fix the problem, altering the focal point farther back on the retina. In farsighted people, the light focuses behind the retina. Glasses with convex lenses can help bring the focal point to the retina.

Lasers

Lasers are another form of light energy. A laser is a narrow, but intense, beam of light. Because of the speed and precision of this energy, lasers are used to cut diamonds and communicate with space satellites. The medical community uses lasers as surgical tools, often aiding in the cutting and repairing of delicate organs.

RELATED READING

- *The Amazing Life of Benjamin Franklin* by James Cross Giblin (Scholastic, 2000).

- *Antoni Van Leeuwenhoek: First to See Microscopic Life* by Lisa Yount (*Great Minds of Science Series*, Enslow, 2001).

- *Brooklyn Bridge* by Lynn Curlee (Atheneum, 2001).

- *Day Light, Night Light: Where Light Comes From* by Franklyn M. Branley (*Let's Read and Find Out Science Series*, HarperCollins, 1998).

- *Engines, Elevators, and X-Rays: The Science of Machines* by Janice Parker (*Science @ Work Series*, Raintree Steck-Vaughn, 2000).

- *Flicker Flash* by Joan Bransfield Graham (Houghton Mifflin, 1999).

- *Forces and Motion* by Peter Lafferty (*Science Fact Files Series*, Raintree Steck-Vaughn, 2001).

- *Inventing the Future: A Photobiography of Thomas Alva Edison* by Marfe Ferguson Delano (National Geographic, 2002).

- *Light and Sound* by Steve Parker (*Science Fact Files Series*, Raintree Steck-Vaughn, 2001).

- *Science of a Light Bulb* by Neville Evans (Raintree Steck-Vaughn, 2000).

- *Science of Noise* by Lynn Wright (Raintree Steck-Vaughn, 2000).

Unit 1 Assessment

Read each statement. Write _T_ on the line if the statement is true. Write _F_ if the statement is false.

_____ **1.** Force is a push but not a pull.

_____ **2.** A flagpole uses a fixed pulley.

_____ **3.** All machines use gear wheels.

_____ **4.** Sound travels faster than light.

_____ **5.** Sound cannot pass through a steel door.

_____ **6.** The bouncing of light off an object is called reflection.

_____ **7.** A shadow has the same shape as the object making the shadow.

_____ **8.** Cardboard is an opaque material.

Darken the letter of the answer that best completes each sentence.

9. A pulley is a wheel with _____.
  Ⓐ a rope that does not move
  Ⓑ an axle attached to it
  Ⓒ a lever attached to it
  Ⓓ a rope that moves around it

10. A _____ is an example of a wheel and axle.
  Ⓐ hammer
  Ⓑ screwdriver
  Ⓒ scissors
  Ⓓ nail

11. A lever can be used to lift a heavy object by _____.
  Ⓐ pushing down on one end of the bar
  Ⓑ pulling the object with the bar
  Ⓒ rolling the object with the bar
  Ⓓ putting the bar on top of the object

12. A wheel reduces friction because _____.
  Ⓐ only a small part of it touches the ground at one time
  Ⓑ it moves slowly
  Ⓒ it is square
  Ⓓ it makes things harder to move

GO ON TO THE NEXT PAGE ☞

13. Sound waves _____.
    Ⓐ move through matter
    Ⓑ spread out in all directions
    Ⓒ start when a vibration is produced
    Ⓓ all of the above

14. Sound is measured in units called _____.
    Ⓐ newtons
    Ⓑ meters
    Ⓒ decibels
    Ⓓ kilograms

15. Deaf persons can tell if a stereo is on because _____.
    Ⓐ they can hear the music
    Ⓑ they can feel the speakers' vibrations
    Ⓒ they can see the sounds
    Ⓓ they see other people sing

16. We can see the Moon because _____.
    Ⓐ it reflects light it gets from the stars
    Ⓑ it makes its own light
    Ⓒ it reflects light it gets from the Sun
    Ⓓ the Earth reflects light from the Sun

17. When light passes through a lens, it _____.
    Ⓐ moves faster
    Ⓑ moves slower
    Ⓒ is bent once
    Ⓓ is bent twice

18. The point where light beams meet after they pass through a lens is called the _____.
    Ⓐ mirror
    Ⓑ prism
    Ⓒ reflection
    Ⓓ focal point

19. How does a prism separate colors?
    Ⓐ It bends each color a different amount.
    Ⓑ It bends each color the same amount.
    Ⓒ It bends only violet.
    Ⓓ It bends only violet and red.

20. Look at the pictures below. Which picture shows how a pencil looks when it is in water?

Ⓐ   Ⓑ

Ⓒ   Ⓓ

Force

A **force** is a push or pull on something. Work is done only when a force moves an object. Forces can make things move and can change the motion of things that are moving. Two or more forces can act at the same time. If the forces act in the same direction, they have greater effect. If they act against each other, they have a lesser effect. Forces can be added and subtracted using the scientific measurement of newtons.

 Use what you know about forces, addition, and subtraction to answer these questions.

100 newtons   75 newtons

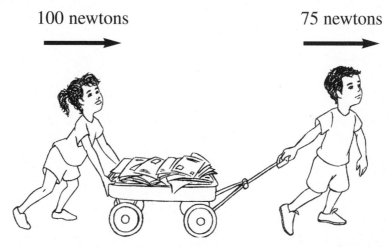

1. Erin and Mikal are trying to move a wagon. Mikal is in front of the wagon and is pulling with a force of 75 newtons. Erin is behind the wagon and is pushing with a force of 100 newtons. What is the total force acting on the wagon? Which way will the wagon move?

   _____

   _____

2. Suppose Erin starts pulling on the back of the wagon with a force of 100 newtons instead of pushing it. Which way will the wagon move? Why?

   _____

   _____

GO ON TO THE NEXT PAGE ☞

Force, p. 2

250 newtons ←   → 260 newtons

Justin's Team   Kate's Team

3. Some students are having a tug-of-war. Justin's team is pulling with a force of 250 newtons. Kate's team is pulling with a force of 260 newtons. Which way will the rope move?

_____

_____

4. Kate is pulling with a force of 60 newtons. But she slips and lets go of the rope. How much force is her team now pulling with? Which way will the rope move? Explain your answer.

_____

_____

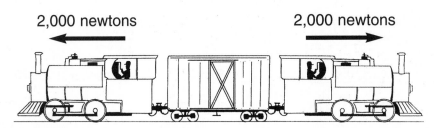

2,000 newtons ←   → 2,000 newtons

5. A locomotive is hooked onto each end of a boxcar. Each locomotive is pulling on the car with a force of 2,000 newtons. Will the boxcar move? Explain your answer.

_____

_____

6. Suppose the locomotive on the left is unhooked from the boxcar. What is the total force on the boxcar now? Which way will the boxcar move?

_____

_____

How Do You Measure Force?

A spring scale measures force. When force is measured, you are actually measuring the weight of an object. Each object pulls on the spring with a force. The heavier the object, or the more force an object pulls with, the more the spring scale will stretch. Force is measured in the scientific unit of newtons. Do this activity to measure force.

You will need

★ spring scale   ★ 3 books of different sizes   ★ string

1. Tie string around the four sides of a book.

2. Lay the scale and book on the floor. Loop the string around the end of the scale.

3. Pull the scale and book straight up. What is the measure of the force?

4. Record the force on the table below.

5. Repeat the steps for the remaining books.

MEASURING FORCE

Book	Force (in newtons)
1	
2	
3	

Answer the questions.

1. Which book needed more force to move? How much force was needed?

_____

_____

2. How did this book compare in size to the other books?

_____

Levers

A **lever** is a simple machine made with a board or bar that moves on a fulcrum. The fulcrum is the turning point for a lever. A lever makes work easier because less force is needed to lift or move an object.

A lever multiplies force. Each picture below shows a tool that is a kind of lever.

 Below each picture, write the name of the tool. Then, write what it does.

1.

Tool: _____

What It Does: _____

_____

2.

Tool: _____

What It Does: _____

_____

3.

Tool: _____

What It Does: _____

_____

4.

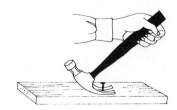

Tool: _____

What It Does: _____

_____

5.

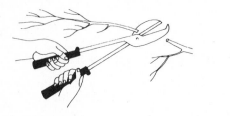

Tool: _____

What It Does: _____

_____

6.

Tool: _____

What It Does: _____

_____

Comparing Forces

It takes force to lift something. The force needed to lift an object is equal to the weight of the object. You can compare the amount of force needed to lift various objects. To do this, you can make a special kind of lever.

You will need
- ☆ shoe box   ☆ quarter   ☆ scissors   ☆ ruler   ☆ penny
- ☆ knitting needle
- ☆ round pencil
- ☆ long cardboard tube (from paper towels or plastic wrap)
- ☆ small objects such as marbles, paper clips, and keys

1. Measure the length of the shoe box. Divide the length by 2 to find the middle of the box. Mark it with your pencil. At the middle, measure 3 cm down from the top of the box. Make a mark, as shown. Do the same thing to the opposite side of the shoe box. The marks should be exactly opposite each other.

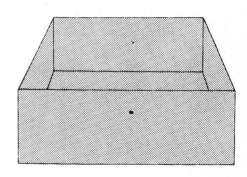

2. Carefully push the knitting needle all the way through the box at both of these marks. Then, take the needle out and set it aside. Now, you have a stand for your lever.

3. Check that the cardboard tube fits lengthwise in the shoe box. If it is too long, cut off enough to make it fit easily.

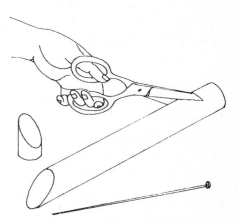

4. Measure the cardboard tube to find the center. At this point, carefully push the needle through both walls of the tube.

5. Cut off the upper part of each end of the tube as shown. Now, you have pans for your lever.

GO ON TO THE NEXT PAGE ☞

Comparing Forces, p. 2

6. Push the needle through the hole on one side of the shoe box, through the cardboard tube, and through the opposite side of the shoe box. Now, you have a lever balance.

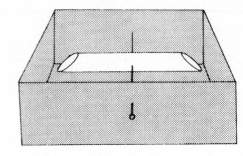

What is the fulcrum? _____

What is the lever? _____

7. Place the quarter in the right-hand pan. What

happens to the tube? _____

_____

What force is pushing the right-hand pan down?

_____

8. Place a penny in the left-hand pan. What happens to the levels of the two pans?

_____

_____

What causes the change? _____

_____

Which exerts more force: the penny or quarter? _____

How can you tell? _____

_____

9. Compare the amount of force applied by the different small objects you collected. Then, make a list of the objects below. At the top of the list, write the object that exerts the most force. At the bottom, write the object that exerts the least force. Write the rest of the objects in order between these two.

_____

_____

Inclined Planes

An **inclined plane** is an example of another simple machine. It is a flat surface that is raised at one end. It is often easier to push something up a ramp than it is to lift the object the same distance because less force is needed. Do this activity to learn more about inclined planes.

You will need

☆ board, 1 m long   ☆ 3 books   ☆ spring scale   ☆ toy truck

1. Place the end of the board on the edge of one book to form an inclined plane.

2. Use the spring scale to pull the truck up the inclined plane. How much force was needed to move the truck? Record your findings on the chart.

3. Set another book under the board to make the angle of the inclined plane steeper. Repeat Step 2.

4. Set the last book under the board to make the angle of the inclined plane steeper. Repeat Step 2.

FORCE ON AN INCLINED PLANE

Number of Books	Force

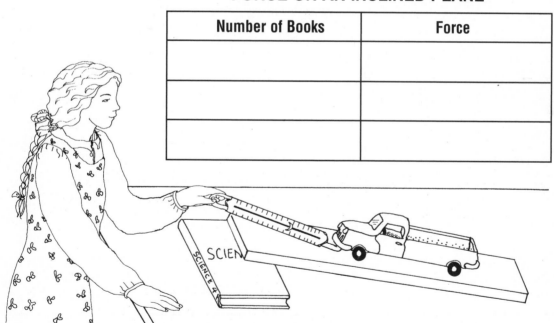

📦 **Answer these questions on another sheet of paper.**

1. Which angle required the most force to move the toy truck?
2. Which angle required the least force?
3. How does the angle of an inclined plane affect the force needed to move an object?

Wedges

A **wedge** is another kind of simple machine. It is formed when two inclined planes join together to make a sharp edge. The force is focused on this edge, making something move apart.

Look at the pictures. Tell what each tool is and how each tool is an example of a wedge.

1.

_____

_____

_____

_____

2.

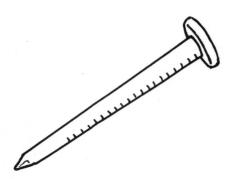

_____

_____

_____

_____

3.

_____

_____

_____

_____

Screws

A **screw** is another kind of simple machine. It is actually made from an inclined plane and a wedge. The point of the screw is the wedge, because it pushes wood or metal apart. The inclined plane is the part formed by the thread. It wraps around the stem of the screw.

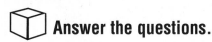 **Answer the questions.**

1. What simple machine is hidden in these two objects?

_____

2. Which of the screws shown below would be the easiest to screw into a piece of

wood? Explain your answer. _____

_____

_____

_____

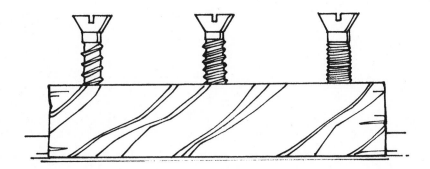

3. In the above pictures, which screw would take the most turns of the screwdriver?

_____

Pulleys

A **pulley** is made by wrapping a rope around a wheel. The wheel has a track around it to hold the rope in place. A pulley that does not move is called a fixed pulley. It makes work easier because it changes the direction of the force. A pulley on a flagpole is a fixed pulley. A movable pulley is fastened to the load. As the rope moves, the pulley and the load both move. It makes work easier by making the force less.

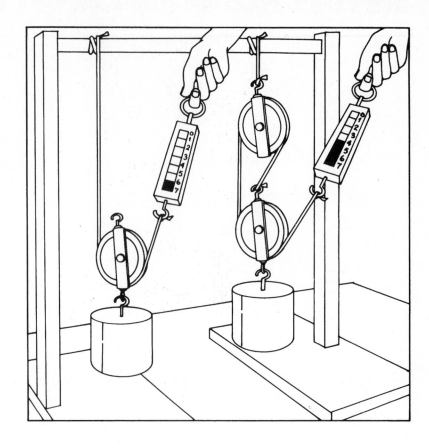

Answer the questions.

1. Which pulley system above makes work easier? Explain.

_____

_____

_____

2. What other objects use pulleys?

_____

_____

How Does a Wheel and Axle Make Work Easier?

A **wheel and axle** is a kind of simple machine. A wheel turns on a rod when force is applied on the wheel. Even though it takes more hand movement to turn the wheel, less force is needed to do the work. Sometimes it is hard to find the wheel and axle in tools. Some examples are screwdrivers, pencil sharpeners, and fishing reels. Learn about a wheel and axle in this activity.

You will need

- ☆ 2 screwdrivers, both the same length but with different-sized handles
- ☆ 2 screws, about 2.5 cm long
- ☆ wood block   ☆ hammer   ☆ permanent marker

1. Put a mark on each of the screwdriver handles.

2. Lightly tap the screws into the wood to set them.

3. Use the screwdriver with the thinner handle first. Turn the screw into the block. Count how many times the handle turns as you turn the screw into the block. Record the number in the chart.

4. Now, use the screwdriver with the thicker handle. Turn the second screw into the block. Count how many times the handle turns as you turn the screw into the block. Record the number in the chart.

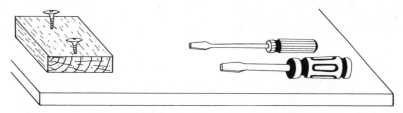

WHEEL AND AXLE TURNS

Type of Screwdriver	Number of Turns
Thinner Handle	
Thicker Handle	

Answer these questions on another sheet of paper.

1. In what part was the wheel?

2. In what part was the axle?

3. Write a paragraph describing the difference between the two screwdrivers. Tell how the difference in their sizes affects the amount of work they can help you do.

How Does a Gear Work?

A **gear** is a wheel with teeth. Usually, several gears work together. When there are large gears and small gears that fit together, they move in opposite directions. The large wheel turns the smaller one. The smaller wheel turns more times and faster than the large gear. An eggbeater is an example of a tool with a small and large gear. Bikes have gears, too. The gears on a bike are connected by a chain. The gears do not touch. They all move in the same direction to make the bike move forward. Do this activity to see how gears work.

You will need

★ eggbeater   ★ dark crayon

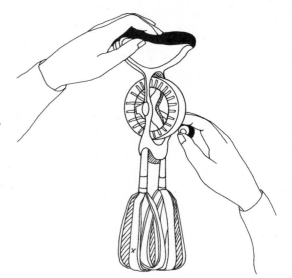

1. With the crayon, put a mark on one blade of the eggbeater.

2. Slowly turn the large gear wheel of the beater one complete turn. Watch the crayon mark. How many turns did the blade make? Record your findings in the chart below.

3. Turn the large gear wheel another complete turn. Then, repeat a third time. Count the times the crayon mark passes each time. Record your findings in the chart below.

TIMES BLADES TURN

Number of Gear Wheel Turns	Number of Blade Turns
1	
2	
3	

Answer these questions on another sheet of paper.

1. How is a gear and wheel system like a wheel and axle system?
2. In an eggbeater, does the blade turn faster or more slowly than the large gear wheel?
3. Use the information in your chart to make a graph of your data.

Friction and Work

Friction is a force that occurs when one object rubs against another object. It keeps objects from moving. Smooth surfaces cause less friction, and rough surfaces increase friction.

 If you wanted to move a heavy crate, which method would you use? List the drawings below in order of decreasing friction.

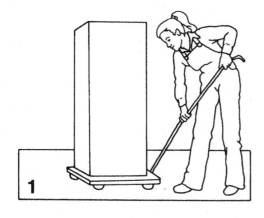 

Order:

_____

_____

_____

_____

 Use the drawings above to answer the questions.

1. In which of the drawings above is the most friction present? _____

2. Which drawing shows the least amount of friction? _____

3. Why do wheels reduce friction? _____

_____

4. Why does a polished floor reduce friction? _____

_____

Do Lubricants Reduce Friction?

In a machine, parts may rub together. A machine is less efficient with friction. A **lubricant** is a material that helps the parts rub across each other more smoothly. Oil is one kind of lubricant. Do this activity to see how lubricants reduce friction.

You will need

★ vegetable oil   ★ 2 marbles

1. Rub your hands together for about 15 seconds. How do your hands feel?

2. Put a small amount of oil in one of your palms. Rub your hands together again. Now how do your hands feel?

3. Wash your hands. Be sure to wash all the oil off.

4. Rub your hands together while holding the marbles. How do the marbles feel in your hands?

5. Put a small amount of oil on the marbles. Rub your hands together while holding the marbles. How do the marbles feel in your hands now?

Answer these questions on another sheet of paper.

1. What lubricant did you use?
2. How did rubbing your hands together with a lubricant compare to not using a lubricant?
3. How did the lubricated marbles feel compared to the marbles that were not lubricated?
4. How does a lubricant affect friction?

How Is Friction Affected by Different Surfaces?

Friction is the force that affects the movement of objects. When two objects rub against each other, friction makes it harder to move them. The surface of the objects affects their movement. Smooth, flat surfaces cause less friction. Objects move more easily across each other. Rough, bumpy surfaces cause more friction. Objects with these surfaces are less likely to move. Do this activity to learn more about surfaces and friction.

You will need

- ☆ small box
- ☆ sand
- ☆ string
- ☆ spring scale
- ☆ sandpaper
- ☆ wax paper
- ☆ tape

1. Fill the box half full of sand.

2. Tie a string around the box. Then, hook the spring scale to the string.

3. Pull the scale to move the box. Record the amount of force needed to move the box on the next page.

4. Put the sandpaper on the table. Tape it to the table. Set the box on it. Pull the box across the sandpaper. Record the amount of force needed to move the box in the chart on the next page.

5. Put the wax paper on the table. Set the box on it. Tape it to the table. Pull the box across the wax paper. Record the amount of force needed to move the box in the chart on the next page.

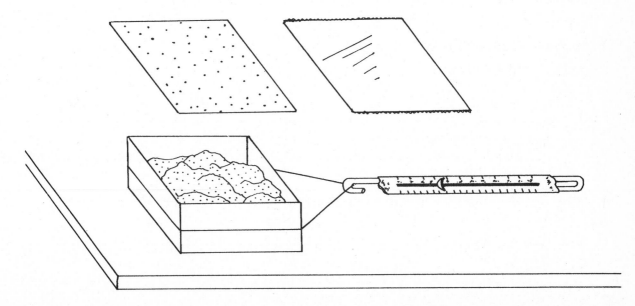

GO ON TO THE NEXT PAGE ☞

How Is Friction Affected by Different Surfaces?, p. 2

SURFACE FRICTION

Surface	Force
Table	
Sandpaper	
Wax paper	

Answer the questions.

1. Over which surface was the most force used? Explain.

_____

_____

2. On which surface was the friction the least?

_____

_____

3. How is friction used to stop a bike?

_____

_____

_____

4. Why do your hands get warm when you rub them together?

_____

_____

_____

Name _____ Date _____

How Do Wheels Reduce Friction?

Wheels help reduce friction because only a small part of the surface rubs against another object. Do this activity to learn more.

You will need

★ shoe box ★ 4 books ★ string ★ spring scale ★ 3 pencils ★ 8 marbles

1. Put all the books in the shoe box.

2. Tie a string around the box. Then, hook the spring scale to the string.

3. Pull the box across the table using the spring scale. Record how much force is needed to pull the box in the chart.

4. Put the pencils under the box. Now, pull the scale to pull the box across the table. Record how much force is needed to pull the box in the chart.

5. Put the marbles under the box. Space them so they are equally spread under the box. Pull the scale to pull the box across the table. Record how much force is needed to pull the box in the chart.

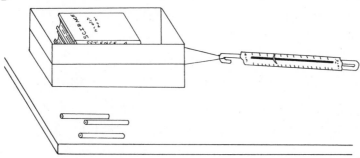

WHEELS AND FRICTION

Surface	Force
Table	
Pencils	
Marbles	

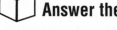 **Answer these questions on another sheet of paper.**

1. What acts like wheels?
2. In which example was friction the greatest? Explain.
3. In which example was friction the least? Explain.
4. List some ways you use wheels every day.

Sound

Have you ever put your hand on a stereo speaker and felt it shake? Stereo speakers and other things that make sounds vibrate. If you pluck a guitar string or tap a tuning fork, you can see it vibrate back and forth. In fact, **sound** travels through the air and other matter as a back-and-forth vibration. You can't see the air around a guitar string or tuning fork vibrate, but if you put a tuning fork in a pan of water, you can see the waves it makes.

 **Circle the best answer to complete each sentence.**

1. Suppose a few grains of rice were sitting on top of a bowl that was covered with plastic wrap. If you held a pan near the rice and hit the pan with a spoon, the rice would _____.
   - Ⓐ rip the plastic wrap
   - Ⓑ fall into the bowl
   - Ⓒ shake
   - Ⓓ soften

2. When you tap a tuning fork, it _____.
   - Ⓐ does nothing
   - Ⓑ makes a sound
   - Ⓒ shakes
   - Ⓓ shakes and makes a sound

3. Another word for shaking back and forth very quickly is _____.
   - Ⓐ spinning
   - Ⓑ twisting
   - Ⓒ sounding
   - Ⓓ vibrating

Suppose some empty glasses are sitting on a table next to a stereo. Explain why the glasses might rattle when someone turns on the stereo.

4. _____

   _____

   _____

   _____

   _____

How Do Sounds Vibrate?

Sound travels in waves. As the waves move out and away from the place where the sound starts, they push against other objects in their path. As the sound wave hits an object, it causes the object to vibrate. The louder the sound, the harder the sound wave hits. Try this activity to learn more about sound.

You will need

☆ plastic bowl   ☆ plastic wrap   ☆ clear tape   ☆ uncooked rice
☆ metal pot   ☆ wooden spoon   ☆ meter stick

1. Stretch the plastic wrap across the top of the plastic bowl. Tape the wrap in place, making sure the wrap is pulled as tightly as it can be.

2. Place the bowl on the table. Place about 20 grains of rice on the plastic so they do not touch.

3. Hold the metal pot near the bowl. Hit the pot with the spoon gently. Then, hit the pot hard. Watch the rice carefully each time. What happens?

4. Hold the pot about one meter from the bowl. Gently tap the pot with the spoon. What happens to the rice this time?

5. Remove the rice. Hold the pot near the bowl again. Rest your fingers lightly on the plastic wrap. Have a classmate gently hit the pot. Then, have your classmate hit the pot harder. Do you feel a difference in the movement of the plastic wrap?

📦 **Answer these questions on another sheet of paper.**

1. What made the rice move?
2. What happened when the pot was hit gently?
3. What happened when the pot was hit hard?
4. How close must the pot be to the bowl to make the wrap move?
5. How can sounds make objects move?

Feeling Vibrations

When you hum, your vocal cords come close together. As your breath moves through your throat, it crosses the vocal cords. This moving stream of air causes your vocal cords to vibrate. You can use this moving stream of air to make other things vibrate, too. Do this activity to see how.

You will need
★ comb   ★ piece of wax paper

1. Fold the wax paper in half. Place it over the comb. Tuck the teeth of the comb into the bottom of the fold.

2. Hum softly without the comb.

3. Then, put the covered comb between your lips. Hum softly again. Does it sound the same as humming without the comb?

Answer the questions.

1. What caused the sound to change when you hummed with the comb?

_____

2. Could you hear the vibrations? Explain. _____

_____

3. Could you feel the vibrations? Explain. _____

_____

Sound in Solids, Liquids, and Gases

Sound can travel through solids, liquids, and gases. However, sound does not travel at the same speed through each kind of matter. Find out more about how sound travels in this activity.

You will need

- ☆ ruler
- ☆ rubber eraser
- ☆ tuning fork
- ☆ water-filled balloon

1. Work with a partner. Stand with your back to your partner. Have the partner strike the tuning fork against the eraser and hold it about 10 cm from your ear. Listen for the sound.

2. Switch places. Repeat Step 1 so that your partner can listen to the sound of the tuning fork.

3. Put your ear against the table. Have your partner strike the tuning fork against the eraser and hold the handle about 20 cm from your head. Listen to the sound. Switch places and repeat.

4. Place the water-filled balloon on the edge of the table. Have your partner strike the tuning fork against the eraser and hold the handle gently to the balloon. (BE CAREFUL NOT TO BREAK THE BALLOON WITH THE TUNING FORK.) Listen for the sound.

📦 **Answer these questions on another sheet of paper.**

1. Did sound travel better through a solid, liquid, or gas? Explain.
2. Through which matter did the sound not move as well? Explain.

Sound and Solids

Sound can travel through a solid object. Does it travel better through some solids than others? Does it travel better through soft materials than hard ones? Do this activity to find the answers.

You will need

☆ pencil   ☆ sponge   ☆ wooden ruler   ☆ metal pot

1. Work with a partner. Press your ear to the surface of a table. Cover your other ear with your hand.

2. Your partner should stand at least one meter from you. Have your partner hold a wooden ruler upright on the table, as shown. Your partner should gently tap the top of the ruler with a pencil.

3. Then, have your partner hold the sponge on the table. Your partner should tap on the sponge with a pencil. Is the sound louder, softer, or the same as when the ruler was tapped?

4. Next, have your partner tap the metal pot with a pencil. Is the sound louder, softer, or the same as when the ruler was tapped?

Answer the questions.

1. Which tapped object was the loudest? _____

_____

2. Does sound travel better through some solids than others? Explain.

_____

_____

3. Does sound travel better through soft objects or hard objects?

_____

Sound Travels at Different Speeds

Sound travels faster through some materials than others. Read the chart below. It shows how fast sound travels through some common materials in one second.

SPEED OF SOUND

Material	Distance Sound Travels in 1 Second
Water	1,433 meters
Steel	4,999 meters
Granite	6,096 meters
Cork	503 meters
Brick	3,627 meters
Lead	1,219 meters
Iron	4,877 meters
Space	0 meters
Air (at 0° C)	332 meters

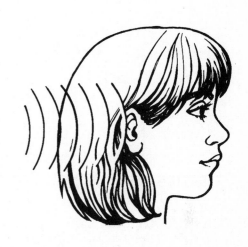

 Answer the questions.

1. Does sound travel through space? _____

2. Of the materials listed, through which does sound move the slowest?

_____

3. Does sound move faster through cork or through water?

_____

4. Of the materials listed, through which does sound travel the fastest?

_____

5. How much faster does sound travel through steel than through iron?

_____

6. How much faster does sound travel through granite than through air?

_____

How Do We Hear?

📦 **The pictures show how you hear a dog when it barks. The sentences tell about the pictures. The sentences are not in the correct order. Write numbers to show the correct order of the sentences.**

_____ The vibrating vocal cords bump the air molecules. These molecules start to vibrate. Sound waves form. They travel from the dog.

_____ The sound waves push against the eardrum and make it vibrate. The vibrating eardrum passes along the vibrations to three tiny bones, a liquid, and thousands of nerve endings.

_____ The dog barks. Its breath passes out of its throat and makes its vocal cords vibrate.

_____ The outer ear collects the sound waves. It brings them into the narrow canal inside the ear.

_____ Messages about the vibrations are sent along a large nerve to your brain. You recognize the sound as barking.

_____ Sound waves from the dog's vocal cords reach your ears.

Inside the Ear

If you tap a tuning fork softly, it makes a soft sound. If you tap it harder, it makes a louder sound. The same thing happens when you pluck a guitar string. The stronger the vibrations, the louder the sound. The sounds of a tuning fork, guitar, or anything else travel out in all directions. By holding a megaphone to your ear, you can focus more sound toward your ear, making the sounds seem louder. In fact, the outer part of the ear is designed to focus sounds into the ear itself. Many animals have ears that help them hear even better than people do. Once sounds enter the ear, they hit a circle of tissue called the eardrum. When the sound waves hit the eardrum, it vibrates and sends signals through the nerves to the brain. The brain interprets these signals as sounds.

Circle the best answer to complete each sentence.

1. If you pluck a guitar string lightly, the sound it makes will be _____.
   Ⓐ loud   Ⓑ soft   Ⓒ high   Ⓓ low

2. To make a guitar sound louder, you need to pluck the string _____.
   Ⓐ faster   Ⓑ slower   Ⓒ harder   Ⓓ softer

3. You can make it easier for someone to hear you if you use a _____.
   Ⓐ megaphone   Ⓑ tuning fork   Ⓒ record player   Ⓓ needle

4. Sounds enter the ear and strike a thin circle of tissue called the _____.
   Ⓐ nerves   Ⓑ brain   Ⓒ cochlea   Ⓓ eardrum

GO ON TO THE NEXT PAGE ☞

Inside the Ear, p. 2

Look below at the diagram of the ear. The captions under the diagram go with the diagram, but they are out of order. Number them so they are in order. Then, decide which part of the diagram each caption describes, and write the number of the correct caption in the circle on the diagram.

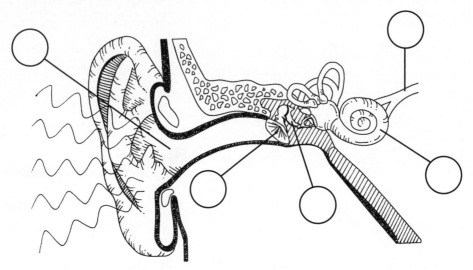

_____ In the cochlea, the vibrations are changed into electric signals.

_____ Sound waves move through the air, hit the outer ear, and are reflected inward.

_____ The electric signals travel through the auditory nerve to the brain, which interprets the signals as sounds.

_____ Within the ear, the sound waves hit a thin circle of tissue called the eardrum, and they make it vibrate.

_____ When the eardrum vibrates, three very small bones move. These bones, in turn, shake the fluid inside a seashell-shaped part of the inner ear called the cochlea.

Making an Eardrum Model

As you may recall, your ear is almost like a megaphone that helps you hear sounds better. As sounds hit your outer ear, they are passed into the inner ear. There they hit the eardrum, which vibrates and sends signals to the brain. Those signals are read by the brain as sounds. You can make an eardrum model in this activity.

You will need

- ☆ soup bowl
- ☆ plastic bag
- ☆ rubber band
- ☆ sugar or rice
- ☆ metal spoon
- ☆ metal sheet or pan

1. Stretch the plastic bag over the mouth of the bowl until the fit is very tight. Put the rubber band around the bowl to keep the plastic in place.

2. Sprinkle a few grains of sugar or rice onto the plastic.

3. Hold the metal pan close to the bowl. Strike the pan with the spoon.

What happens?

_____

_____

_____

_____

 Answer these questions on another sheet of paper.

1. How is the model you made like an eardrum?
2. When you hear a sound, what is happening?
3. How does the vibrating sugar show that sound waves travel?
4. If you were deaf and looking at the model of the eardrum you just made, how could you tell the loudness of a sound someone made nearby?

Decibels

Roaring, humming, honking, giggling . . . sounds are all around us. Sounds can be pleasing, like a cat purring when you stroke it. And sounds can be annoying, like a phone ringing and ringing. But sounds can also be damaging. Noise can make your head hurt and make you feel bad all over. Very loud sounds can damage your ears and can even make you lose your hearing.

Sound is measured in units called **decibels**. Decibels begin at 0 for sounds that a human with normal hearing would not be able to hear. Something very quiet, such as whispering, is about 10 decibels. As sounds get louder, the number of decibels gets higher. At a certain point, sounds become so loud that they are felt as pain rather than heard as sounds. The chart below shows some common sound levels.

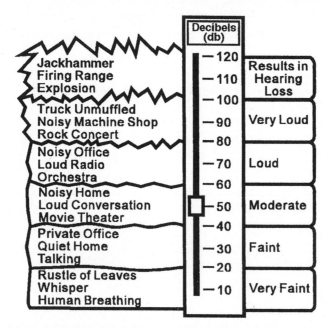

 Study the decibel table above. Use it to answer these questions on another sheet of paper.

1. Sounds that are 100 decibels or higher can cause hearing loss. What sounds might damage hearing?

2. What is an example of a sound that is as quiet as whispering?

3. How much louder than whispering is talking?

4. How many decibels do you think a shout would be?

5. What is an example of a sound that is heard at a moderate noise level? How many decibels does this sound measure?

6. Make a bar graph of common sounds. Use the data given in the table. You may also add data that you find in reference books.

Echo Sounder

Sound waves can be used to map the bottom of the ocean. An **echo sounder** is a scientific instrument that sends out sound waves from a ship. The sound waves travel through water until they hit the bottom of the ocean. Then, they bounce back to the ship. The time that it takes the sound waves to travel to the ocean bottom and return is measured. Since scientists know how fast sound waves travel in water, they can calculate how far it is to the bottom of the ocean. When sound waves return quickly, it shows that the land is high and there may be a mountain. Sound waves that take a long time to return show that the ocean is deep. There may be a trough.

The line graph below shows an echo sounder reading of an ocean bottom.

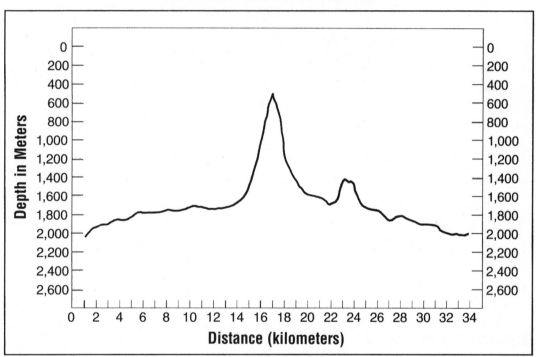

ECHO SOUNDER READING

 Study the line graph. Use it to answer these questions on another sheet of paper.

1. How do scientists map the bottom of the ocean?
2. What distance did the scientists map on this chart?
3. At what depth is the top of the underwater mountain?
4. How deep is the deepest part of the ocean shown in the chart?
5. From the deepest part of the ocean, how high is the underwater mountain?
6. What are some other reasons that scientists would use an echo sounder to explore the ocean bottom?

Light Sources

Light is a form of energy made by the Sun, the stars, light bulbs, fires, and fireflies. We can see other objects because the light from a light source bounces off, or reflects off, an object and hits our eyes. The Moon is an example of reflection. Light from the Sun hits the Moon and bounces back so we can see it.

Look at the objects below. Write *light source* or *reflects light* to tell which objects give off light.

1. _____   2. _____   3. _____

4. _____   5. _____   6. _____

Can You See a Light Beam?

You need light to see. If there is no light, you cannot see. And while you can get along without being able to see, it is not easy. In order for you to see something, there must be light shining on it. The light reflects off, or bounces off, the object and travels to your eyes. This reaction is similar to the way a ball bounces off a wall. Try this activity to see a light beam.

You will need

☆ flashlight   ☆ spray bottle filled with water

1. Find a room in which no light can enter. Turn off the lights. What do you see?

2. Turn on the flashlight. Shine it across the room. What do you see?

3. Spray some water where you think the light beam is.

Answer the questions.

1. When you turned on the flashlight, did you see a light beam?

_____

2. What made the light beam visible? _____

3. How does the water help you to see the light beam? _____

_____

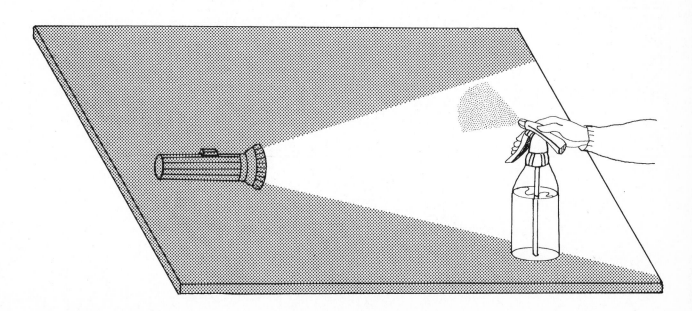

Does Light Travel in a Straight Line?

Like sound, light moves out in all directions from its source. It moves very fast. If something blocks the light, the light is reflected back. The blocked object makes a shadow behind. A shadow is a dark place that has the shape of the object. Because of the shadows, we know that light travels in a straight line. You can do this activity to prove it.

You will need

★ 3 index cards   ★ clay   ★ flashlight   ★ ruler

1. With the index cards held together, punch a hole through them. Make sure the hole is in the same spot on each.

2. Place clay balls in a straight line about 5 cm apart from each other.

3. Stick a card in each ball. Try to line up the holes.

4. Shine the light through the holes. Hold your hand open behind the last card.

5. Slide the second card to one side. What do you see?

 Answer these questions on another sheet of paper.

1. Did the light travel through the holes when they were lined up?
2. What happened to the light when you moved the middle card?
3. When did you see shadows? Explain.
4. Does light travel in a straight line? How do you know?
5. What happens to light when it is blocked by an object?

When Light Strikes

You can tell whether an object is transparent, translucent, or opaque by the type of shadow it casts. A **transparent** object casts no shadow. Light passes right through it. An **opaque** object casts a sharp shadow. All the light is blocked by the object. A **translucent** object casts a blurred shadow. Some of the light is blocked or scattered as it passes through.

You will need

- ☆ set of 4 clear plastic glasses
- ☆ water
- ☆ waxed paper
- ☆ brown wrapping paper
- ☆ flashlight
- ☆ blue food coloring
- ☆ permanent marker

1. Label the glasses *1, 2, 3,* and *4.* Leave glass 1 empty. Add water and blue coloring to glass 2. Wrap the brown paper around glass 3. Wrap the waxed paper around glass 4.

2. Shine the flashlight beam at each glass. Observe what kind of shadow forms. Record your observations in the chart below.

SHADOWS OF OBJECTS

Glass	Shadow Formed	Object Is
1		
2		
3		
4		

 Answer the questions.

1. Which object(s) is transparent? _____

2. Which object(s) is translucent? _____

3. Which object(s) is opaque? _____

Reflecting Light

You cannot see someone who is hiding around a corner, even though you may be able to hear the person. Light travels in a straight line; but with a mirror, you can see someone hiding around the corner. When light hits a mirror, it bounces off and changes direction. Do this activity to learn more about reflecting light.

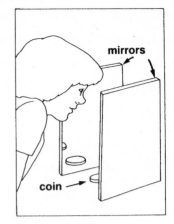

You will need

☆ 2 mirrors   ☆ a coin   ☆ tape

NOTE: This activity must be done with an adult.

1. Stand the two mirrors on edge facing each other. Place the coin between the mirrors. Look in one mirror. Then, look in the other mirror. What do you see?

2. Hinge the two mirrors together with a piece of tape. Set them on edge at an angle to each other. Place a coin between the two mirrors. Observe the number of images formed as you increase and decrease the angle between the mirrors.

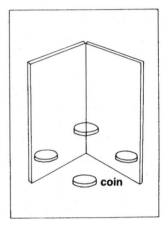

Answer the questions.

1. How many images did you see in the mirror in Step 1?

_____

2. How many images did you see in Step 2?

_____

3. What happened as you increased the angle?

_____

_____

Bouncing Light

When a beam of light hits an object that reflects, the beam bounces off, or reflects, at the same angle it hits, if the surface is smooth. However, if the surface is uneven, the light bounces off in many different angles. The drawings below show how light reflects off a smooth surface and an uneven surface.

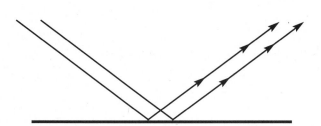 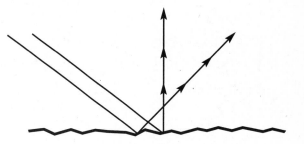

 Complete each drawing below to show the path of light after it is reflected.

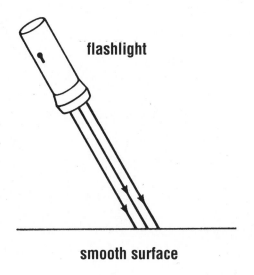

smooth surface

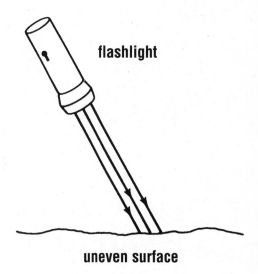

uneven surface

How Can Flat Mirrors Focus Light?

Some mirrors are curved. Though they are shiny and the surface is smooth, their shape causes light beams to bend at different angles. Curved mirrors are like many flat mirrors joined together to make a curve. Mirrors that curve inward can focus light. This means that the light beams are bent, or reflected, so that they hit the same spot. Do this activity to see how flat mirrors focus light.

You will need

- ✦ light box or flashlight
- ✦ 3 small mirrors
- ✦ black paper
- ✦ 5 x 7-inch index card
- ✦ clay
- ✦ ruler

1. Place the sheet of black paper about 40 cm from the flashlight.

2. Make a screen of the index card by bending the long edge. Place it beside the black paper.

3. Turn on the flashlight and darken the room.

4. Use clay to stand one mirror in the light.

5. Turn the mirror so that the light is reflected on the index card.

6. Place a second mirror next to the first. Turn it so that it reflects light onto the same place on the index card.

7. Using the last mirror, repeat Step 6.

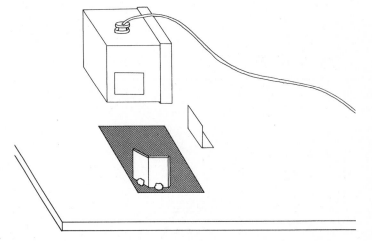

 Answer these questions on another sheet of paper.

1. What happened to the light hitting the index card when the second mirror was added?

2. What happened when the third mirror was added?

3. How can flat mirrors be used to focus light?

4. How can several flat mirrors be used to act like one curved mirror?

Curved Mirrors

Curved mirrors are like flat mirrors joined together. When light hits, it reflects at different angles. Mirrors that curve inward are **concave mirrors**. They reflect light so that it is focused in one spot. Images reflected in the concave mirrors look larger. The inside of a spoon is an example of a concave mirror. **Convex mirrors** curve outward. The reflected light scatters out in a semicircle, making images look smaller. A flashlight has a concave mirror. Security mirrors that hang near the ceiling of stores are convex mirrors.

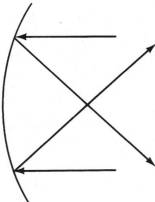 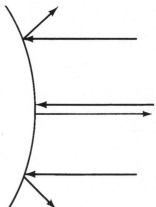

 **Answer the questions.**

1. What is the difference between a convex mirror and a concave mirror?

_____

_____

_____

2. How is a curved mirror used in a flashlight?

_____

_____

_____

3. How is a convex mirror used in a store?

_____

_____

_____

Curved Mirrors, p. 2

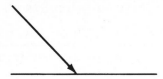 **Light bounces off flat and curved surfaces. In each of the diagrams below, show the path of the reflected beam of light.**

4.

5.

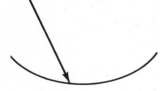

6.

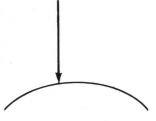

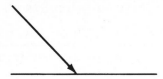 **Answer the questions.**

7. Name an instrument that uses each of the above mirrors.

_____

_____

8. Which of the above mirrors might be used in a fun house?

_____

9. Which mirror would be used in a car headlight to make a beam of light?

_____

_____

How Can You Bend a Light Beam?

Light can travel through some objects. When light passes from one material to the next, it bends. The kind of material the object is made of slows the speed of light. Because of the change in speed, light is bent. If you have ever seen a straw in a clear cup of water, the straw looks as if it is broken. The speed of light as it passes from air to water changes, making the straw look as if it is cut in half at the water's surface. Do this activity to bend a light beam.

You will need

- ☆ light box or flashlight
- ☆ water
- ☆ black paper
- ☆ clear, plastic shoe box
- ☆ milk
- ☆ spray bottle

1. Place the shoe box on the black paper. Fill the shoe box with water.

2. Mix 4 or 5 drops of milk in the water.

3. Shine the light through one long side of the shoe box.

4. Spray some water in the beam of light. Look down from above. What do you see?

5. Try to bend the light by moving the flashlight to a new position. What happens now?

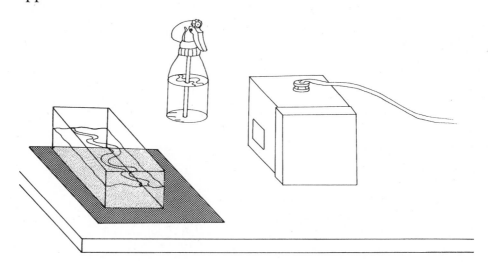

Answer these questions on another sheet of paper.

1. What happens to the light beam when the flashlight points straight to the side of the shoe box?

2. If you change the angle of the flashlight, what happens?

3. What can you change to make the light beam bend even more?

Lenses Bend Light

A **lens** is a piece of curved glass or plastic material that bends light beams. The distance from the center of the lens to the point where the light beams meet is the **focal length**. The angle that a beam bends depends on the shape and the thickness of the lens. A thicker lens will have a shorter focal length. When the light enters one side of the lens, it bends as it passes from air to glass or plastic. It bends a second time as the light leaves the glass and enters the air.

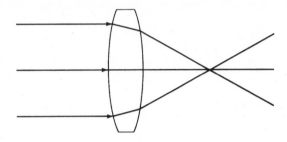

Answer the questions.

1. How is a lens like a curved mirror?

_____

_____

_____

2. Why are lenses made of transparent materials?

_____

_____

3. How does a lens bend light?

_____

_____

_____

4. Name three objects that use lenses.

_____

_____

How Glasses Work

Have you ever heard the term *nearsighted*? A person who is nearsighted has trouble seeing things far away but has no problem seeing things that are nearby. A person who is *farsighted* has the opposite problem and has trouble seeing things that are close.

What causes a person to be nearsighted or farsighted? Both problems may be caused by the shape of the eye or by problems in the cornea or the lens. In normal vision, light rays travel from an object to a person's eye. In the eye, the light rays pass through the cornea and the lens. These two parts of the eye bend the light rays together and focus them on the retina at the back of the eye. An image of the object forms on the retina. Look at the drawing to see how this happens.

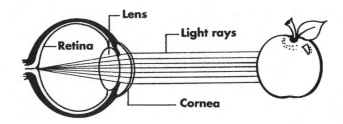

When a person has vision problems, it is often because light is not being focused onto the correct spot inside the eye. If a person is nearsighted, the light rays come together, or focus, before they reach the retina. A person is usually nearsighted because his or her eyeballs are a little too long. This vision problem can be corrected with glasses that change the place where the light rays come together. These glasses have concave lenses. A concave lens is thinner in the middle than it is on the edges.

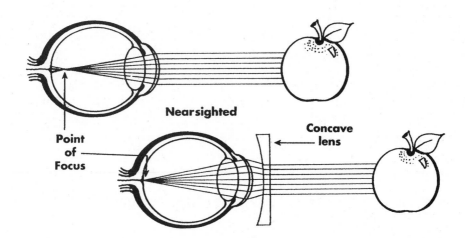

GO ON TO THE NEXT PAGE 🖝

How Glasses Work, p. 2

When a person is farsighted, the light rays focus on a spot beyond the retina. This may be because the eye is a little too short. When people get older, they often become farsighted because the lenses of their eyes are no longer able to focus as well as when they were younger. Farsightedness can be corrected with glasses that have convex lenses, which are thicker in the middle than on the edges. These glasses also change the point at which light rays come together.

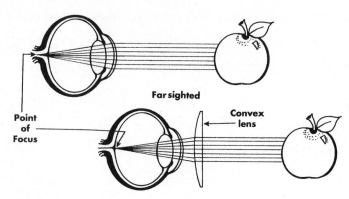

Answer the questions.

1. Explain how light is focused for normal vision.

_____

_____

_____

2. Explain how light is focused in the eyes of people who are nearsighted and people who are farsighted.

_____

_____

_____

3. How does the shape of the lenses in glasses help correct vision problems?

_____

_____

_____

White Light and Prisms

Light that comes from a natural source is **white light**. When it passes into glass or water, the speed slows and the beam bends. White light that enters a **prism**, a triangular piece of glass, bends in the glass, and then bends again when leaving the glass. The result is a spectrum, seven colors that make up light. The colors are red, orange, yellow, green, blue, indigo, and violet. The color red bends the least in a prism, while violet bends the most.

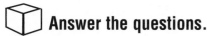 **Answer the questions.**

1. What happens when white light passes through a prism?

_____

2. What is a spectrum?

_____

_____

3. How is a raindrop like a prism?

_____

_____

4. How is a rainbow made?

_____

_____

_____

What Happens When Light Hits an Opaque Object?

White light is made up of seven colors. When the light hits an object, all the colors in the white light hit the object, too. If all the colors bounce off, the object looks white. In colored objects, that color of the white light is reflected back to our eyes. As a result, we can see that color. All the other colors soak into, or are absorbed by, the object. For example, we see a blue ball because the blue light in the spectrum reflects to our eyes. The other colors are absorbed, so we cannot see them. To learn more, do this activity.

You will need
⭐ white, red, green, blue construction paper   ⭐ flashlight

1. Lay the white paper on a table. Turn on the flashlight. Darken the room.

2. Hold a sheet of colored paper at an angle to the white paper.

3. Shine the flashlight onto the colored paper. Gradually change the angle of the colored paper, making it smaller. What do you see on the white paper? Record your findings in the chart.

4. Repeat Steps 2 and 3 with the other colors of paper.

COLOR REFLECTION

Color of Paper	Color of Reflection
Red	
Green	
Blue	

Answer these questions on another sheet of paper.

1. What is white light?

2. What color was reflected onto the white paper from each of the three sheets of colored paper?

3. What happened to the other colors that make up the white light of the flashlight?

4. What happens to light when it hits an opaque object?

Seeing Colors

You can make a color wheel to learn more about how we see color. Here's how.

You will need

- ★ 9-cm cardboard circle
- ★ red, green, and blue crayons
- ★ 1.5 m (5 ft.) of string
- ★ hole punch

1. Divide the circle into three equal sections as shown in the drawing.

2. Using the crayons, color one section red, the second blue, and the third green.

3. Punch two small holes in the wheel about 3 mm (0.1 in.) on each side of the center. See the drawing.

4. Pass the string through the two holes as shown. Tie the ends.

5. Turn the wheel to twist the string. You can now spin the wheel by pulling the string in and out. (This may take some practice.)

Answer the questions.

1. What happens to the colors as the wheel spins?

_____

2. What color do you see?

_____

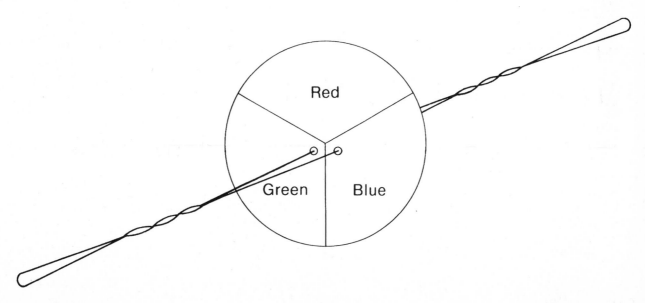

Red

Green   Blue

Using Lasers

A **laser** produces a very narrow beam of intense light. When you shine a flashlight across a room, the beam has spread out by the time it reaches the wall. If you direct a laser across a room, its beam will be the same size on the wall as it was at the source. The energy in a laser beam can be used to cut through metal. A laser beam has many other uses, too.

Some lasers are entertaining, like the spectacular sight of a laser light show. If you watched a light show that used ordinary light, it might not be very exciting. By the time the light got to the sky, it would be so spread out that you would not be able to see it. Because a laser beam is so concentrated, however, you can see it far up in the sky.

Laser beams help doctors perform many operations. For example, before laser surgery was developed, doctors had to use knives to cut into the eyeball to repair damage. Now, laser beams allow doctors to direct a tiny beam of light that can heal the damage without cutting the rest of the eye. Some dentists use a laser instead of a drill to remove tooth decay.

You may have a compact disc (CD) player at home. If you do, you own a laser. In a CD player, the laser beam reflects off the shiny disc. The reflection is turned into a signal that becomes sound when it goes through the speakers. Videodiscs also use lasers. With videodiscs, though, the signals are also converted into a picture that appears on a TV screen.

Many supermarkets now have lasers at checkout counters to read the prices on items. The laser beam moves over the bar code (the block of thin black lines, or bars) on packages. It reads those bars, and up pops the price.

Answer the questions.

1. How is the beam from a laser different from a flashlight beam?

_____

_____

2. Why would someone who runs a store want to use a laser to record the prices of items when a customer checks out?

_____

_____

_____

Name _____ Date _____

Special Effects

Glass can reflect light and also let it pass through. You can use this fact to make special effects. You can make a candle appear to burn in a glass of water.

You will need

- ☆ piece of clean glass at least 20 cm x 25 cm
- ☆ 2 thick books, about the same size
- ☆ tall, clear plastic tumbler
- ☆ candle in a small candleholder
- ☆ 2 sheets of paper
- ☆ tape   ☆ water   ☆ ruler   ☆ matches

NOTE: This activity must be done with an adult.

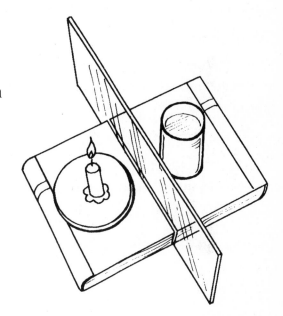

1. Tape the edges of the glass. Stand the piece of glass between the two thick books, as shown. Place a sheet of paper on top of each book. Make sure the paper is pushed right up against the edge of the glass.

2. Fill the tumbler with water. Place it in the center of one of the books.

3. Put the candle and holder on top of the other book.

4. Using your ruler, measure how far the tumbler is from the glass. Place the candle the same distance from the glass.

5. Have your teacher light the candle. Turn out the lights and pull down the shades.

6. Look at the tumbler of water through the glass. DO NOT GET CLOSE TO THE CANDLE. Move around slowly until you see a reflection. What do you see?

📦 **Answer these questions on another sheet of paper.**

1. What do you see when you complete Step 6?
2. Why do you think it happens?
3. How is the glass a reflector?
4. What other image do you see when you look in the glass?
5. Why can you see another image?

Unit 2: Earth and Space Science

BACKGROUND INFORMATION

The Earth is made up of three materials: solids, liquids, and gases. The solids inside the Earth are such things as minerals, rocks, and soil. The liquid with which we are most familiar is water. But the Earth also has liquid metal and rock under its surface. And various gases, mostly oxygen and nitrogen, make up the atmosphere that allows life on the Earth.

The Earth

The Earth has a diameter of about 8,000 miles (12,900 km) and a circumference of about 25,000 miles (40,250 km). The Earth is made up of three layers. The outer layer of the Earth, called the crust, is quite thin, ranging from three to 34 miles (5–55 km) thick. We live on the crust, and most of the rocks and minerals we recognize come from the crust.

Below the crust is the mantle. The mantle is about 1,800 miles (2,900 km) thick, and it is made of mostly solid rock. The mantle is very hot, up to 5,400°F (3,000°C). Below the mantle is the core. The core is about 2,200 miles (3,500 km) thick, and it has a temperature as high as 7,200°F (4,000°C). Most scientists think the core has two parts, an outer core and an inner core. The outer core is made of melted iron and nickel. The inner core is a solid ball of iron and nickel.

Minerals and Rocks

Rocks are made up of minerals. Minerals have four characteristics.
1. They are substances that occur naturally.
2. They are inorganic solids.
3. Minerals of the same type usually have the same chemical composition.
4. The atoms of minerals are arranged in a regular pattern that forms crystals.

Rocks are classified into three basic groups: igneous, sedimentary, and metamorphic. These groups are based on how the rock is formed.

Igneous rocks begin as molten rock, a red-hot liquid. *Igneous* means "fire," so igneous rocks can be called "fire rocks." After a long while, the molten rock cools and hardens to form solid rock. The hardening can occur on the surface or below the surface of the Earth. Molten rock that is on the surface of the Earth is called lava. Granite is an example of igneous rock.

Sedimentary rocks are made up of sediments, or bits of rock and sand. The sediments piled up to form layers. The weight of the layers squeezed the sediments. Chemicals in the sediments cemented them together. The squeezing and cementing eventually caused the sediments to harden into layers of rock. Sandstone is an example of sedimentary rock.

Sometimes rocks that have already formed become buried deep in the Earth. There, great pressures inside the Earth squeeze the rocks. Great heat makes the rocks very hot, but does not melt them. The squeezing and heat slowly change these rocks from one kind to another. The new kind of rock is called a metamorphic rock. *Metamorphic* means "changed." Igneous, sedimentary, and even other metamorphic rocks can be changed to form new metamorphic rocks. Slate is an example of metamorphic rock. Slate is formed from the sedimentary rock shale.

Soil

Soil is the grainy material that covers much of the land on the Earth. Soil is made of tiny bits of rock, minerals, organic materials, water, and air. Soil is needed for life to exist on the Earth. Plants need soil to grow. Then, animals, including people, eat the plants to stay alive.

Soil is created through a long process. Rocks break down through weathering and erosion into a stony product called parent soil. This type of soil is broken down further, mostly through weathering. Organic matter called humus mixes with the parent soil. When the long process is complete, the rock bits and humus have mixed to produce fertile soil, which is good for growing plants.

The Earth's Surface Changes

The Earth's surface undergoes constant change. Some of this change is very slow and gradual. Other changes are rapid and violent. Some of the slow processes are weathering and erosion, and the rapid changes are associated with earthquakes and volcanoes.

Weathering and Erosion

Any process that causes rocks or landforms to break down is called weathering. Weathering is caused by several agents, including water, wind, ice, and plants. Weathering is usually a slow process, causing the gradual deterioration of the rocks or landforms.

Erosion is another way in which rocks and landforms are broken down or worn away. Erosion is the process in which weathered rock and soil are moved from one place to another. The most effective agents of erosion are moving water, waves, gravity, wind, and glaciers.

Earthquakes and Volcanoes

A much more violent process can change the landscape in only a few minutes. These rapid changes are produced by the actions of earthquakes and volcanoes. Earthquakes and volcanoes can change the landscape quickly, and they can also cause great damage to property and human life. Earthquakes can cause great splits in the ground, or large sections of the Earth can be pushed upward. Buildings can be damaged or even knocked down by the shaking that earthquakes cause. The lava flow of a volcano can damage the area around the volcano. The volcano's ash cloud can cause health hazards for people, and it can even alter the weather. Sometimes volcanoes explode. When this happens, everything nearby is flattened or burned.

To understand earthquakes and volcanoes, you must understand the structure of the Earth's crust. Scientists now believe that the Earth's crust is broken into about ten pieces, called plates. These plates move. Scientists believe that at one time in the very distant past, all the continents were joined. The continents were on some of these plates. Over time, the plates moved apart, causing the continents to move apart, or drift. A look at a world map will show how this theory is possible.

Scientists believe the plates can move in three ways. These movements occur at the boundary lines between the plates. These boundary lines are called faults. When two plates push against each other, they collide. The thin part of one plate slowly pushes its way under the thick part of another plate. The upper plate then rises. This is how some mountains are formed. Earthquakes are also common where plates collide.

Two plates can move apart, causing magma (molten rock) to squeeze up between the plates. The magma then cools and hardens into new crust. Volcanoes and earthquakes are very common where plates move apart.

Two plates can also slide past each other, causing a great grinding. The San Andreas Fault in California divides two plates. One is called the North American Plate, and the other is the Pacific Plate. These two plates slide against each other often, so earthquakes are common in California.

Fossils

A fossil is the preserved remains of a thing that was once alive, usually a plant or an animal. These remains are found in rock layers, so that if scientists know how old the rocks are, they can tell how old the plant or animal is. Scientists who study fossils are called paleontologists.

Most fossils form from a bone or a shell. Some fossils, though, mark the burrow or track of an animal; these are called trace fossils. Most fossils are found in sedimentary rock. But fossils have also been found in asphalt, frozen ice, and tree resin.

Energy

People on the Earth need great amounts of energy to cool, heat, and light their homes. They also need energy to run their machines and automobiles. Much of this energy comes from fossil fuels such as oil, gasoline, coal, and natural gas that formed over long periods of time from the remains of once-living plants and animals.

But other sources of energy, often called alternate energy, are now used more and more. Solar power can cook food, dry clothes, and produce electricity. Wind power and water power are also used to produce electricity. As fossil fuel supplies deplete, these alternate types of energy will become more necessary.

Water

Water is our most precious resource. Water covers about 70 percent of the Earth's surface. Without water, life could not exist. Our bodies are about 65 percent water. We use water in many ways. Water is an amazing substance, too. It can be a solid, a liquid, and a gas. It can change from a solid state (ice) to a liquid state (water) to a gaseous state (water vapor) and back again.

The Water Cycle

Water often changes from its liquid form to its gaseous form and back to its liquid form in a process called the water cycle. The three main steps in the water cycle are evaporation, condensation, and precipitation. Evaporation is necessary to get the liquid water into its gaseous form of water vapor in the air. Condensation is needed to turn the vapor back to a liquid in the clouds. And precipitation returns the liquid water to the Earth.

Evaporation occurs as liquid water is heated and changed into water vapor. The water vapor is then carried up into the sky by rising air. Condensation takes place as the rising water vapor cools and is changed into liquid water, forming clouds. Precipitation happens as water droplets grow heavy and fall to the Earth as rain, snow, or some other type of precipitation.

Gases and the Atmosphere

We live on the crust of the Earth. We have food and water. But another part of the Earth's structure is necessary to sustain life. That part is called the atmosphere. The atmosphere is made up of various gases, mostly nitrogen and oxygen, that allow us to survive on the Earth. The atmosphere is about 500 miles (800 km) high, and it is held in place by the Earth's gravity.

The atmosphere has four layers. Closest to the Earth is the troposphere, the layer in which we live. The troposphere is only a thin band, about five to ten miles (8–16 km) thick. All the Earth's weather occurs in the troposphere. The troposphere also contains the air we need to live. The air in the troposphere is about 80 percent nitrogen and 20 percent oxygen. There are also small amounts of other gases, including argon and carbon dioxide.

Above the troposphere is the stratosphere, a layer that is from about five to 50 miles (8–80 km) high. The stratosphere has only a few clouds, which are mostly made of ice crystals. In the stratosphere are the fast moving winds known as the jet stream. The air in the lower part of the stratosphere is cold. In the upper part of the stratosphere, the temperature increases. The important ozone layer is in the upper stratosphere. The ozone absorbs ultraviolet energy from the Sun, which causes the temperature there to rise. The ozone layer is important because it protects creatures on the Earth from the harmful ultraviolet rays.

Above the stratosphere is the ionosphere, which stretches from about 50 miles to about 300 miles (80–500 km) above the Earth. There is almost no air in the ionosphere. But the ionosphere is useful for radio astronomy and communication with satellites. The natural displays of light called auroras occur in the ionosphere.

The top layer of the atmosphere is called the exosphere. It begins about 300 miles (500 km) above the Earth, but it has no definite top boundary. This layer is the beginning of what we call outer space. The exosphere contains mostly oxygen and helium gases. This layer also has a very high temperature, up to several thousand degrees.

Weather

Weather, in its most basic explanation, is caused by the uneven heating of the Earth's surface by the Sun. The land and the water are heated differently. This uneven heating causes pockets of air with different temperatures. Cool air is heavier than warm air. As a result, the cooler air moves under the warmer air, so the lighter warm air is pushed up. This movement of air causes winds. These factors all work together to produce weather.

As you recall, we live in the layer of the Earth's atmosphere called the troposphere. Air in the troposphere moves constantly. The air is heated, not directly by the Sun, but by the air's contact with the Earth. Air closer to the Earth is warmer than air higher up. Cold air is heavier than warm air, so the cold air moves downward. The warm air rises as it is displaced, setting up the patterns of air circulation in the troposphere.

Near the Earth's surface, the sinking air results in high-pressure zones, called ridges. The rising air results in low-pressure zones, called troughs. The differences in air pressure produce winds. Wind moves out of high-pressure zones in a clockwise direction and into low-pressure zones in a counterclockwise direction. Weather data identifies winds by the direction from which they come. For example, a wind moving toward the south is called a north wind, because north is the direction from which it comes.

Great air masses move slowly across the Earth's surface. These moving air masses take on the characteristics of the surface beneath them. Air moving over a warm surface is warmed, and air moving over a cold surface is cooled. Air moving over water becomes moist, and air moving over land becomes drier. As it moves, the air mass causes changes in the weather of an area.

Fronts

A front is a line or boundary between air masses. The air masses clash along the front, so weather along a front is often stormy. A cold front occurs when a cold air mass replaces a warm air mass. Weather along a cold front often includes thunderstorms with much precipitation. A warm front occurs when a warm air mass replaces a cold air mass. Precipitation may also occur along a warm front, but the precipitation is usually not as heavy as along a cold front. A stationary front occurs when air masses meet without moving. A stationary front may produce an extended period of precipitation.

Precipitation

Precipitation is one of the most obvious features of weather. As you recall, precipitation is the third step in the water cycle, following evaporation and condensation. Sometimes precipitation does not fall in an area for a long period of time. Plants and crops can die, and sometimes even animals and people die as a result of the lack of water. When an area does not receive precipitation for a long time, it is said to be in a drought.

Clouds

Another of the most obvious, and sometimes most spectacular, features of weather is the cloud. Clouds can take several forms, from thin and wispy to dense and billowy. How do clouds form? Remember the movement of air, with warm air rising as the cold air sinks? First, through evaporation, water on the Earth's surface becomes water vapor in the air. As the warm air rises and expands, it naturally begins to cool. Water vapor in the air starts to condense around tiny particles in the air, such as dust or smoke, forming droplets. Clouds form in different shapes, depending on their height, the coolness of the air, and the amount of water vapor in the air.

The water droplets grow bigger as more water vapor condenses. When the droplets get so large they cannot be held up by the rising air, they fall as rain or some other form of precipitation. If the cloud is cold and contains crystals of ice, snow may fall instead of rain.

There are three main types of clouds: cirrus, cumulus, and stratus. Cirrus clouds are high above the Earth and are usually seen in fair weather. These clouds, made of ice crystals, are wispy and streak the sky. Cumulus clouds are white and fluffy, looking much like cotton balls. They are often seen in good weather, though they can produce rain showers or snow. Stratus clouds are low, dark clouds close to the Earth. They often produce rain or snow.

Stormy Weather

Weather comes in many forms, fair and foul. Fair weather includes sunny days, gentle breezes, and mild temperatures. But foul weather is more spectacular, accompanied as it often is by powerful displays of wind, rain, lightning, and thunder. One of the most common examples of foul weather is the thunderstorm. Approaching thunderstorms are often accompanied by towering cumulus clouds called thunderheads. These billowy clouds have flat tops and dark bottoms. Thunderheads are formed when warm, moist air rises. As the rising air begins to cool, water vapor in the air condenses, and cumulus clouds form. The hot ground causes the heated air to rise faster and higher. The cumulus clouds grow larger and taller, often reaching ten miles or more (16 km or more) into the air. As the clouds grow in size, they become more likely to produce rain.

Thunderheads also produce two well-known features of stormy weather: lightning and thunder. Lightning is an electrical spark caused by friction inside the thunderhead. As the clouds grow, raindrops scrape against each other, and friction is produced. This friction builds up an electrical charge, just as you do when you scrape your feet across a carpet. Most of the electric charges in the lower part of the cloud are negative. These negative charges emit a spark that jumps toward a positive charge on the ground. This spark is what we call lightning. The lightning instantly heats the air around its path. This heated air expands quickly and collides with cooler air. The collision between the heated air and the cooler air produces the sound we know as thunder.

The Sun

Life on the Earth begins with the Sun, and the Earth's weather is also caused by the Sun and its energy. The Sun produces energy in the form of heat and light. In the center of the Sun, its core, nuclear fusion reactions change hydrogen into helium. These reactions release an unbelievable amount of energy. At the core, the Sun burns at a temperature of about 27 million degrees F (15 million degrees C). The energy moves from the core to the surface of the Sun, which has a temperature of almost 4 million degrees F (2.2 million degrees C). The energy then travels through space as electromagnetic waves of light and heat.

The Earth is 93 million miles (150 million km) from the Sun, so only a tiny amount of the Sun's energy reaches the Earth. But this small amount is enough to sustain life and create weather on the Earth. Much of the Sun's energy and harmful rays are filtered out by the Earth's atmosphere. About half of the Sun's energy is absorbed or reflected by the ozone, clouds, or the air. About 50 percent is absorbed by the Earth's surface.

The Sun is much larger than the Earth, with a diameter of about 840,000 miles (1,352,400 km), compared to the Earth's diameter of about 8,000 miles (12,900 km). But the Sun is, in fact, only a medium-sized star. Many early people believed that the Sun moved around the Earth, but the opposite is true. The Earth orbits around the Sun, once every 365 days or 1 year.

The Solar System

The Earth joins eight other planets in the solar system. These nine planets orbit around the Sun. (Recent research by astronomers suggests there may be a tenth planet somewhere beyond Pluto.) They all receive energy from the Sun, but they receive varying amounts based on their distance from the Sun. The inner planets (Mercury, Venus, Earth, Mars) receive more energy because they are closer. The outer planets (Jupiter, Saturn, Uranus, Neptune, Pluto) are very cold planets where the chance of life is very small. Students can remember the order of the planets outward from the Sun by using this saying: "My Very Energetic Mother Just Sent Us Nine Pizzas."

Most of the other planets are quite different from the Earth. The planet closest to the Sun, Mercury, has a year, or one orbit of the Sun, that is only 88 Earth days long. On Mercury, the surface temperature can be as low as about −290°F (−173°C) or as high as 800°F (500°C). For the most distant planet, Pluto, one orbit takes 248 Earth years. Pluto is about three billion miles (4.8 billion km) from the Sun. On Neptune, winds sometimes blow up to 700 miles per hour (1,125 km per hour).

The planets are held in their orbits by the Sun's gravitational pull. Likewise, the Earth and the farther planets have smaller bodies, or moons, that orbit around them, held by each planet's gravitational pull. The Earth has one moon. On the other hand, Jupiter has at least 17 moons.

The Moon

The Moon is a satellite of the Earth. It is about one fourth the size of the Earth, with a diameter of about 2,100 miles (3,400 km). The Moon appears about the same size as the Sun in the sky, but that is only because the Moon is so much closer than the Sun. The Moon is about 240,000 miles (384,000 km) from the Earth, and the Sun is about 93 million miles (150 million km). The Moon orbits the Earth once about every 28 days.

The Moon has no light of its own, but it seems to shine because it reflects the Sun's light. The Moon also has no atmosphere and no life. The Moon's gravity is only about one sixth as strong as the Earth's gravity. A person who weighs 60 pounds (27 kg) on the Earth would weigh only 10 pounds (4.5 kg) on the Moon!

Meteors

Have your students ever seen a "shooting star"? Shooting stars are not really stars; this is just a popular name for meteors. Comets leave behind a trail of dust and gas, also called meteoroids, as they pass through the solar system. When the Earth moves through these dust particles, they appear in our atmosphere as meteors. Because most meteors are no bigger than a grain of sand, they burn up quickly in a flash of light. If a meteor is large enough, it may survive its dive and hit the surface of the Earth. Then, the surviving chunk of rock is called a meteorite.

The Earth passes through the same fields of comet dust every year. This passage produces yearly showers of meteors, from several to hundreds of meteors per hour. Some of the more spectacular meteor showers are the Quadrantids on January 3, the Perseids on August 12, and the Geminids on December 14.

Comets

Perhaps your students have heard of Halley's Comet, which makes an orbit near the Earth about every 76 years. Comets are chunks of ice and rock that were left over when the solar system formed. Comets move around the Sun in oval-shaped orbits. Some comets take only three years to complete their orbits, and others take millions of years. The most unusual feature of a comet is its tail. As a comet nears the Sun, part of the comet begins to melt and turn to vapor. This process causes a long, visible gas tail to stream behind the comet. The tails of comets always point away from the Sun.

Phases of the Moon

The Moon revolves around the Earth, causing the Moon's phases. The Moon has no light of its own; it only reflects the Sun's light. This reflected light is visible from the Earth in different amounts during periods called phases. When the Moon is between the Sun and the Earth, only the Moon's side away from the Earth is lit. The side facing the Earth is unlit; this phase is called the New Moon.

A little more of the Moon becomes visible each day after the New Moon phase. At first, a small crescent of light appears on the Moon's eastern edge; this is called a crescent Moon. This crescent grows larger each day. A week after the New Moon phase, half of the Moon facing the Earth is lighted; this phase is called the First Quarter. After another week, the Earth is between the Sun and the Moon; all of the Moon facing the Earth is lighted. This phase is called the Full Moon. Though the phase is called the Full Moon, the Moon is only truly fully lighted on one night. Between the New Moon and Full Moon phases, the Moon is said to be waxing.

A week after the Full Moon phase, only half of the Moon facing the Earth is lighted. This phase is called the Last Quarter. Another week later, the Moon returns to the New Moon phase. Between the Full Moon phase and the return to the New Moon phase, the Moon is said to be waning.

The complete cycle of phases for the Moon takes about 29.5 days. The phases are caused by the Moon's changing position in relation to the Earth and the Sun. Because the Earth blocks sunlight from reaching parts of the Moon, only those lighted parts of the Moon are visible from the Earth.

Eclipses

Sometimes the Sun, the Earth, and the Moon line up on the same plane. During this time, eclipses occur. In a lunar eclipse, the Moon becomes darkened by the Earth's shadow. In a solar eclipse, the Moon prevents sunlight from reaching a small amount of the Earth's surface.

A lunar eclipse takes place when the Earth is directly between the Sun and the Moon. The Moon slowly moves into and out of the Earth's shadow. A lunar eclipse can only occur during a full Moon, and the eclipse lasts a few hours. Looking directly at a lunar eclipse is not harmful.

A solar eclipse occurs when the Moon is directly between the Sun and the Earth. Then the Moon's shadow falls on a part of the Earth's surface. If the Sun seems to be completely covered by the Moon, this is called a total eclipse. A total eclipse lasts only about eight minutes. Most solar eclipses, though, are partial. Only a part of the Sun appears to be covered. Looking directly at a solar eclipse is a very bad idea; you can severely damage your eyes.

RELATED READING

- *Asteroid Impact* by Douglas Henderson (Dial Books for Young Readers, 2000).

- *Cloud Dance* by Thomas Locker (Silver Whistle/Harcourt, 2000).

- *Comets and Asteroids* by E. M. Hans (*Spinning Through Space Series*, Raintree Steck-Vaughn, 2001).

- *The Drop in My Drink: The Story of Water on Our Planet* by Meredith Hooper (Viking, 1998).

- *Earthquakes* by Sally M. Walker (*Earth Watch Series*, Carolrhoda Books, 1996).

- *A Handful of Dirt* by Raymond Bial (Walker, 2000).

- *Mary Anning: Fossil Hunter* by Sally M. Walker (Carolrhoda Books, 2000).

- *Planet Earth* by David Jefferis (*Record Breaker Series*, Raintree Steck-Vaughn, 2003).

- *Weather Explained: A Beginner's Guide to the Elements* by Derek M. Elsom (*Your World Explained Series*, Henry Holt, 1997).

- *Weather Watch: Forecasting the Weather* by Jonathan D. W. Kahl (*How's the Weather? Series*, Lerner, 1996).

Unit 2 Assessment

Read each statement. Write *T* on the line if the statement is true. Write *F* if the statement is false.

_____ 1. The Earth's core is very cold.

_____ 2. Fossils are pictures of plants and animals that are alive now.

_____ 3. Weathering is the breaking down of rocks.

_____ 4. Precipitation can take the form of rain, hail, sleet, or snow.

_____ 5. Dark surfaces reflect a lot of sunlight.

_____ 6. The planet closest to the Sun is Mars.

Match each term with the correct statement. Write the letter of the term on the line.

a. sedimentary rocks	**b.** oil	**c.** precipitation	**d.** lava
e. crust	**f.** orbit	**g.** metamorphic rocks	**h.** solar system
i. faults	**j.** troposphere	**k.** igneous rocks	**l.** condensation

_____ 7. You are on this part of the Earth.

_____ 8. These rocks are "formed by fire."

_____ 9. The Sun, the Earth, and the other planets form this.

_____ 10. Rain and snow are examples of this.

_____ 11. Sandstone is one of these.

_____ 12. This is an example of a "fossil fuel."

_____ 13. Earth's weather occurs in this layer of the atmosphere.

_____ 14. The Earth moves around the Sun in this path.

_____ 15. This molten rock breaks through the Earth's surface.

_____ 16. Clouds are formed in this part of the water cycle.

_____ 17. These are breaks in layers of rock.

_____ 18. These are rocks that are "changed in form."

GO ON TO THE NEXT PAGE ☞

Unit 2 Assessment, p. 2

☐ **Darken the letter of the best answer.**

19. The mantle of the Earth is made of _____.
- Ⓐ mostly solid rock
- Ⓑ wood
- Ⓒ dust
- Ⓓ nickel and iron

20. What changes in a rock during physical weathering?
- Ⓐ color
- Ⓑ size and shape
- Ⓒ the inside of the rock
- Ⓓ nothing

21. Erosion occurs when _____.
- Ⓐ soil is added to the ground
- Ⓑ dams are built
- Ⓒ rocks and soil are carried away by wind and water
- Ⓓ grass and trees are planted

22. The change in water from a liquid to a gas is called _____.
- Ⓐ condensation
- Ⓑ evaporation
- Ⓒ rain
- Ⓓ snow

23. Water vapor changes into a liquid when the air gets _____.
- Ⓐ wetter
- Ⓑ cooler
- Ⓒ warmer
- Ⓓ drier

24. The layer of air that we breathe is the _____.
- Ⓐ stratosphere
- Ⓑ ionosphere
- Ⓒ hemisphere
- Ⓓ troposphere

25. The two main gases in air are oxygen and _____.
- Ⓐ water vapor
- Ⓑ nitrogen
- Ⓒ hydrogen
- Ⓓ magma

26. The movement of air from high pressure zones to low pressure zones is called _____.
- Ⓐ sediment
- Ⓑ thunder
- Ⓒ wind
- Ⓓ carbon dioxide

27. For a solar eclipse to occur, what has to happen?
- Ⓐ The Moon has to pass between the Earth and the Sun.
- Ⓑ The Earth has to pass between the Moon and the Sun.
- Ⓒ The Sun has to pass between the Earth and the Moon.
- Ⓓ The Moon has to be full.

28. Of the following, which planet takes the most time to revolve around the Sun?
- Ⓐ Mercury
- Ⓑ Pluto
- Ⓒ Earth
- Ⓓ Venus

Inside the Earth

The Earth has three layers. Can you name the parts of the Earth shown in this diagram?

◻ **Study the table and the clues below to help you. Write the name of each layer on the line.**

Layer of Earth	Thickness
crust	5–55 km
mantle	2,900 km
core	3,500 km

1. _____ →

2. _____ →

3. _____ →

Clues:

1. The layer of the Earth that is 5–55 km thick.
2. The layer that is mostly solid rock and is 2,900 km thick.
3. The layer deep inside the Earth. It is made of nickel and iron.

◻ **Can you compare an apple with the Earth? On another sheet of paper, draw a picture of an apple. Compare the following parts of the apple to the layers of the Earth: the skin of the apple, the fleshy part of the apple, and the apple's core.**

Rocks That Change

Igneous rocks form from cooling lava and magma. **Sedimentary rocks** form from layers of sediment at the bottom of lakes and oceans. These rocks form under great pressure and often contain remains of dead plants and animals. **Metamorphic rocks** form from other rocks.

Read the following sentences about different kinds of igneous and sedimentary rocks. Use clues from each sentence to decide if the rock described is igneous or sedimentary. Then, write *igneous* or *sedimentary* on the line.

1. Sandstone is made mainly of grains of quartz that are cemented together. When sandstone breaks, it splits between the grains. Much sandstone was formed in layers in shallow seas. It often contains fossils.

_____

2. Obsidian is a black, glossy rock formed when lava has cooled quickly.

_____

3. Bituminous coal is soft and dull. It forms from the remains of dead plants and animals that have been changed by great pressure.

_____

4. Granite contains feldspar and quartz minerals. The minerals are in a light and dark pattern that looks like mixed salt and pepper. It forms from magma that has cooled slowly beneath the Earth's surface.

_____

Read these sentences about metamorphic rocks. Each formed from a rock described above. Use the clues to decide from which sedimentary rock each rock came. Then, complete the sentence at the end of each description.

5. Quartzite has tiny grains that are cemented together. In fact, the "cement" is stronger than the grains. When quartzite breaks, it breaks across the grains rather than in the cement between them.

Quartzite came from the sedimentary rock _____.

6. Anthracite coal is shiny and hard. It is made of the remains of dead plants and animals that have been changed by heat and pressure.

Anthracite coal came from the sedimentary rock _____.

Making Sedimentary Rocks

Time relationships tell you about the order of events. Space relationships tell you about locations of objects. Understanding these relationships can help you make accurate models.

Some sedimentary rock layers form from sediments that are mixed with ocean water. Suppose you wanted to find out how these layers form. You break up a lump of clay into tiny pieces. You drop the pieces into a jar of water and put the lid on the jar. Then, you shake it until the clay is mixed with the water. You place the jar on a table. The water-and-clay mixture is cloudy and gray. Five minutes later, you look at the jar. Almost all the clay has settled in a layer at the bottom of the jar. You measure the height of the clay layer and record its height in a chart. You check the jar every 5 minutes for another 20 minutes. Each time, you measure and record the height of the clay. The results of your experiment are shown in the chart.

MAKING ROCKS

Number of Minutes	5	10	15	20	25
Height of Clay	3 cm	5 cm	6.5 cm	7.5 cm	8 cm

 Answer these questions on another sheet of paper.

1. What was clay a model of in your experiment?
2. What time interval were you using in the experiment? What were you relating to time in your experiment?
3. What was the difference in the height of the clay for each measurement?
4. Suppose you were to make a measurement 5 minutes after the last measurement in the table. About how much higher would you expect the clay layer to be? Explain your answer.
5. What conclusion can you draw about how sediments in ocean water form rock layers over time?
6. How can you use recognizing time relationships to make good decisions about the relationship of your observations to the amount of time between them?

Rock Facts

Read these statements about rocks. Then, circle the kind of rock that the statement describes. Each statement may be true of more than one kind of rock.

KINDS OF ROCK

1. They come in many shapes and sizes.

   (igneous) (sedimentary) (metamorphic)

2. These rocks form when volcanoes erupt.

   (igneous) sedimentary metamorphic

3. These rocks often contain fossils.

   igneous (sedimentary) metamorphic

4. Nearly everything solid in the Earth's crust is made of these rocks.

   (igneous) (sedimentary) (metamorphic)

5. Lava and magma cool to form these rocks.

   (igneous) sedimentary metamorphic

6. Metamorphic rocks come from these rocks.

   (igneous) (sedimentary) metamorphic

7. This name means "formed by fire."

   (igneous) sedimentary metamorphic

8. Shells of sea animals can form these rocks. Example: Fossil

   igneous (sedimentary) metamorphic

9. This name means "changed in form."

   igneous sedimentary (metamorphic)

10. Lake and ocean bottoms are where these rocks have their beginnings.

    igneous (sedimentary) metamorphic

11. Erosion can wear away these rocks.

    (igneous) (sedimentary) (metamorphic)

12. The imprint of an insect may appear in these rocks. Ex: fossil

    (igneous) (sedimentary) metamorphic

13. The pressure of layers of sediment helped form these rocks.

    igneous (sedimentary) (metamorphic)

Heating and Cooling

Rocks are worn down by wind and rain. Plants and freezing water split them apart. Heating and cooling also affect rocks. You can find out how.

You will need

☆ 4 glass marbles	☆ paper towel	☆ small pan	☆ potholder
☆ hand lens	☆ small tin can	☆ heat source	☆ water
☆ ice cubes	☆ safety goggles		

1. Using a hand lens, examine the marbles.

   Do you see any cracks? _____

2. Put two ice cubes into the can. Cover the ice cubes with cold water. Put the can aside.

3. Place the marbles in the pan. Have your teacher help you heat them for three minutes.

4. Use the potholder to tip the pan so that the hot marbles fall into the ice-cold water. Set them aside for three minutes.

5. Using the same marbles, repeat steps 3 and 4 three more times. Add more ice cubes to keep the water in the can cold.

6. Remove the marbles from the water. Dry them with a paper towel. Look at them under the hand lens. What happened to them?

🔲 Answer the questions.

1. How are the Earth's rocks heated and cooled?

_____

_____

2. How does repeated heating and cooling change the rocks?

_____

_____

Growing Crystals

One feature of minerals is that they are made of **crystals**. What's the world's most tasty mineral? Some would say salt. Salt is interesting to look at, too. It forms clear crystals that are almost perfect cubes. You can see them if you look at some table salt under a magnifying glass. Salt crystals dissolve when you stir them into water, but you can make the salt turn into crystals again. Here's how.

You will need

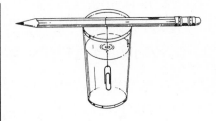

- ☆ clear glass
- ☆ box of salt
- ☆ measuring tablespoon
- ☆ string or thread (15 cm long)
- ☆ pencil
- ☆ hot tap water
- ☆ cup
- ☆ spoon for stirring
- ☆ paper clip
- ☆ tape

1. Fill the glass with hot water from the tap. An adult may help you do this part of the activity.

2. Pour salt into your empty cup. Add one tablespoon of the salt at a time to the hot water. Stir well after each addition until all the salt is dissolved. Keep doing this until no more salt will dissolve. Set the glass aside.

3. Tie one end of the string to one end of the paper clip. Tie the other end of the string to the middle of the pencil. Tape the string in place on the pencil, if necessary.

4. Lay the pencil over the top of the glass. The paper clip should hang down into the water. It should not touch the sides or bottom of the glass.

5. Observe the glass for several days. Do not move or touch it.

Answer these questions.

1. What do you see happening in the glass? _____

_____

_____

2. Why have the crystals formed? _____

_____

_____

Minerals in Soil

There are minerals in soil that come from weathered rocks and decayed plant materials. These minerals are necessary for plant growth. Because the minerals may be dissolved in the soil or the particles are very small, we cannot see them. You can try the following activity to see some of the minerals found in the soil.

You will need

☆ baby-food jar   ☆ garden soil   ☆ large shallow dish   ☆ distilled water

1. Fill the jar with soil.

2. Pour in enough distilled water to cover the soil.

3. Screw on the lid and shake.

4. Allow the jar to stand overnight so that the soil will settle to the bottom.

5. Carefully pour off the water into a large shallow dish.

6. Allow the dish to remain undisturbed for several days until the water evaporates. Examine the material that is left in the dish. Minerals remain that were present in the soil.

Answer the questions.

1. Explain why distilled water was used. _____

_____

_____

2. Where did the minerals in the dish come from? _____

_____

_____

3. How can you use the minerals in the dish for an experiment on plant growth?

_____

_____

_____

Soil Profiles

Different areas have different types of soil. The formation of soil is affected by many different factors. Since soil is formed from rock, the kind of rock available affects soil type. Soil also contains decayed plant and animal matter. Therefore, living things in that area affect soil type. Climate and topography affect soil type as well.

 **Use a reference book to help you match the following words about soil with their meanings. Write the letter of the correct meaning on the line.**

_____ **1.** loam   **a.** the layer of leaves on top of the soil

_____ **2.** leaf litter   **b.** small rock particles

_____ **3.** leaf mold   **c.** a layer where lime minerals collect

_____ **4.** sand   **d.** loose soil material made of fine particles

_____ **5.** silt   **e.** soil made up of decayed plant material, clay, and sand

_____ **6.** lime layer   **f.** the layer of decaying leaves under leaf litter

A **soil profile** is a cross section of soil from the surface down to the bedrock. Columns A and B, shown on the next page, are soil profiles. These are cross sections of soils from two different places in the United States.

Answer the questions.

7. Which profile column has a greater depth of decayed plant material?

_____

8. Which profile column shows an area where minerals carried from the surface collect at lower depths?

_____

GO ON TO THE NEXT PAGE ☞

Soil Profiles, p. 2

9. Which of these profile columns might be found in an area of forest?

_____

Why? _____

_____

10. Which soil might be best for farming? _____

Why? _____

_____

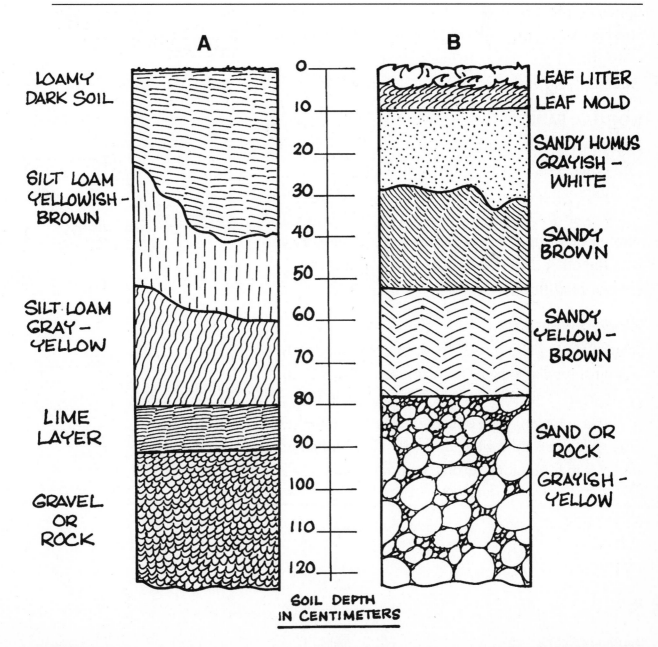

A

LOAMY
DARK SOIL

SILT LOAM
YELLOWISH-
BROWN

SILT LOAM
GRAY-
YELLOW

LIME
LAYER

GRAVEL
OR
ROCK

B

LEAF LITTER
LEAF MOLD

SANDY HUMUS
GRAYISH-
WHITE

SANDY
BROWN

SANDY
YELLOW-
BROWN

SAND OR
ROCK

GRAYISH-
YELLOW

0
10
20
30
40
50
60
70
80
90
100
110
120

SOIL DEPTH
IN CENTIMETERS

Faults and Earthquakes

Faults are breaks in the Earth's crust. The rock walls on either side of a fault can slip past each other when forces in the Earth move them. This movement is a major cause of **earthquakes**.

The three major kinds of faults are lateral faults, normal faults, and reverse faults. The difference between these faults is the way in which the rock walls move past each other.

LATERAL FAULT

Pressures under the Earth's surface sometimes push pieces of the crust that are next to each other in opposite directions. When this happens, rock walls slip sideways past each other. This is a lateral fault. California's San Andreas Fault is a lateral fault. It extends 1,167 km (725 mi) through the state.

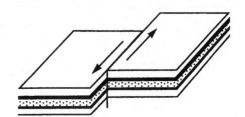

NORMAL FAULT

Forces within the Earth can push some rock up and pull other rock down on the Earth's surface. Eventually, the rock breaks, forming a normal fault. Rock walls pull away from each other along a normal fault line. One of the walls slides downward past the other. Mountain ranges can form along normal fault lines.

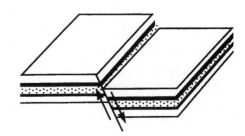

REVERSE FAULT

In addition to pulling rock apart, forces in the Earth can push rock together. This also causes the rock to break apart. This action forms a reverse fault. Rock walls push toward each other along a reverse fault line. One wall slides upward against the other. Mountain ranges can form along reverse fault lines, too.

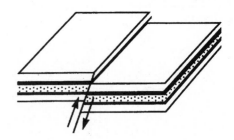

GO ON TO THE NEXT PAGE ☞

Faults and Earthquakes, p. 2

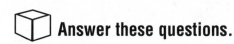 **Answer these questions.**

1. Explain how mountains like these might form along a fault line. What type of fault would help shape these mountains?

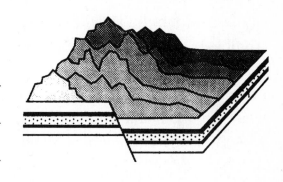

_____

_____

_____

_____

_____

2. What is the difference between a normal fault and a reverse fault?

_____

_____

_____

_____

3. Explain how a fault could have caused this curb to break. What type of fault would cause it?

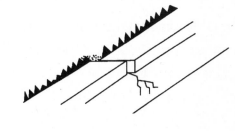

_____

_____

_____

_____

_____

_____

Mount St. Helens

May 18, 1980, was unusually quiet. The birds did not sing. The squirrels did not chatter. Even the leaves did not rustle. Suddenly, two huge earthquakes broke the stillness. Mount St. Helens shook. Solid earth crumbled. The slopes of the mountain gave way. An avalanche of mud and dirt slid into the valley below. Long cracks opened in the ground. Hot gases trapped inside the mountain exploded out through the cracks. The north side of the mountain blew off!

Broken rock and dust rose 19 km into the air. A huge, dark cloud formed that seemed to turn day into night. Thunder rumbled. Lightning flashed. A powerful shock wave spread out from the peak. In less than a minute, the shock wave knocked down millions of trees that had stood in its path.

Hot gases instantly melted the ice and snow on the slopes. The melted water mixed with soil, rock, and falling volcanic ash. Gigantic rivers of boiling mud rushed into the streams and rivers around Mount St. Helens. One mud flow plunged into the Toutle River. Pushing the water over the banks, it created an instant flood. The mud and flood waters washed away bridges, uprooted trees, and killed animals.

The eruption changed the shape of Mount St. Helens. Its ridges and valleys will never be the same. From time to time, the mountain still throws out hot gas and ash. No one knows if Mount St. Helens will ever be peaceful again.

📦 **Write the correct answer to complete each sentence.**

1. Before Mount St. Helens erupted on the morning of May 18, 1980, the mountain

slopes were unusually _____.

2. The May 18th eruption began with two _____.

3. Trapped gases exploded out of _____.

4. A _____ knocked down millions of trees.

5. Water, rocks, soil, and ash mixed to form hot _____.

Moving Continents

Scientists believe the continents were once all joined. Over time, they drifted apart. What do you think? Try the activity below to see if the scientists might be right.

You will need

- ☆ 1 sheet of construction paper
- ☆ 1 sheet of tracing paper
- ☆ scissors
- ☆ paste
- ☆ this map of the world

1. Place the tracing paper on top of the map.

2. Trace the border around the outline of each continent.

3. Trace the outline of each continent within its border.

4. Cut out each tracing along its border. Be careful when using the scissors.

5. Put the cutouts on a piece of construction paper. Try to fit the continents together.

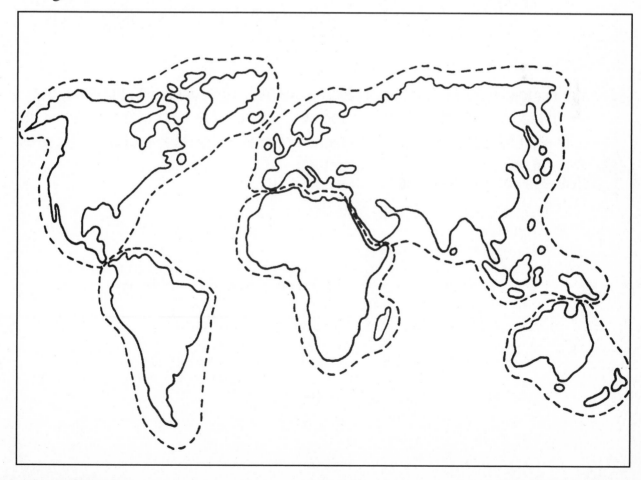

Fossils of the Future

Rain and moving water wear away rocks. They wash sand and mud into lakes and oceans. Slowly, layers of sediment build up on lake bottoms and ocean floors.

When animals and plants that live in oceans and lakes die, they sink to the bottom. Soft parts of their bodies are eaten by other animals or rot away. Hard parts, such as shells and bones, remain. New layers of sediment bury these hard remains.

After millions of years, layers of sediment will become thick and heavy. The bottom layers, under great pressure, harden into sedimentary rock. The shells and bones trapped inside turn to stone, too. These **fossils** will take millions of years to form.

The sentences below tell how a fossil is formed. The sentences, however, are not in the correct order. Read the sentences. Write *1* in front of the sentence that tells what happens first. Then, continue to write numerals to indicate the correct order of events.

_____   Dead animals sink to the bottom of the ocean.

_____   Sediment hardens into rock.

_____   Layers of sediment bury hard parts such as shells and bones.

_____   The soft parts of the dead animals are eaten or rot away.

_____   Rain and moving water wash sand and mud into the ocean.

_____   Hard shells and bones turn to stone.

Where Does Oil Come From?

Have you ever heard the term *fossil fuel*? It means a source of energy that comes from once-living things. You know about such fossils as dinosaur bones. Those fossils are bones that over a long period of time turned to stone. Just as those bones turned to stone, other bones turned to oil. **Oil** is made of bones and tree trunks and shells and all sorts of other parts of organisms that lived thousands and even millions of years ago.

When living things die, they are broken down and covered over by dust, soil, or sand. As they are covered over by other layers of once-living things and by more layers of soil, sand, and rock, they get buried deeper and deeper below Earth's surface. These "sandwiches" of once-living things, sand, and soil are eventually subjected to very high pressure and to very high temperature. When the pressure is great enough, the sand and soil change into rock. And at just the right temperature, the once-living things change into a liquid called oil and a gas called natural gas.

After oil and gas form, other layers of rock continue to press down from above, causing still more pressure. This pressure causes the rock to go even deeper into the Earth. But this pressure on the oil and gas is like pushing a balloon under water; it just tends to pop back up again. The oil and gas move upward through cracks and holes in the rock. One kind of rock, called reservoir rock, contains many small holes, or pores. Oil and gas are often found in this porous rock. Finally, the oil and gas are stopped from moving upward by other, nonporous layers of rock. Then, the oil and gas pool in a trap, where the oil may remain until it's discovered and the rock is drilled to extract it.

You may wonder how people find oil. In the past, oil was often found accidentally. There were many areas where oil traps lay close to the surface. In these areas, if someone dug a deep hole in the ground, the digger might reach the oil trap. Once a hole was made into the trap, gas and oil would shoot out and up into the air. Many oil wells in Texas were accidentally discovered in this way.

People use oil quickly, and much of the oil found in traps lying close to the surface has been used up. Researchers must now find oil that lies deeper in the Earth. These oil and gas reserves are often found by identifying the type of rock in which they might be found. Scientists have discovered that different types of rock reflect sound in different ways. By thumping the Earth and then measuring the echo, they can find rock that might contain oil and gas.

GO ON TO THE NEXT PAGE ☞

Where Does Oil Come From?, p. 2

As more and more oil is used up, scientists have begun looking beneath the ocean floor for oil traps. Since the ocean is so huge, there might be vast amounts of oil and gas buried under the water. But here it is difficult, expensive, and dangerous to remove the oil. Sometimes the oil is found in somewhat shallow water not far from the coast, and drilling platforms can be anchored to the ocean floor. When the oil is under deeper water, different types of drilling platforms operate while floating in the water. If the trap is below very deep ocean waters, it must be reached and removed by vessels called drill ships. In contrast, oil under land is reached by much simpler drills and is then pumped out of the ground. Another factor that makes drilling underwater more difficult and more expensive is that all the ocean sites must be reached either by ship or by helicopter.

Answer these questions.

1. How do oil and gas form? Why are they called fossil fuels?

_____

_____

_____

2. You have read that some oil traps on land shoot out oil and gas. What do you think might happen if an oil well deep under the ocean suddenly began to shoot out oil? How might it affect people working on the rig? How might it affect ocean life?

_____

_____

_____

3. What do you think? Is ocean drilling a good idea? Is it worth the dangers? Explain.

_____

_____

_____

Coal

Coal is an important fuel. It burns well and gives off a lot of heat. People have used coal for cooking and heating for hundreds of years.

Coal is a black rock that began as dead plant material and formed in the following way. Dead plant material piled up in swampy places over millions of years. Mud and dirt covered the decayed plants. The weight of the upper layers pressed down on the lower layers. Water was squeezed out of the dead plant material. The material became rock in the steps shown:

⟶ **INCREASING AGE OF ROCK** ⟶

PEAT	LIGNITE	BITUMINOUS	ANTHRACITE
first step in coal formation	brown coal	soft coal	hard coal
provides low heat; not really coal	provides low heat; low sulfur content; small supply in most areas	provides high heat; high sulfur content; large supply; often used as a fuel	provides high heat; low sulfur content; small supply in most areas; best type of coal for fuel

⟶ **INCREASING HEAT PRODUCED BY BURNING** ⟶

The United States is one of the world's largest coal producers. Most of this coal is bituminous. Seventy percent of the coal mined in the United States is burned in energy plants to make electricity. Much of the rest is made into coke, which is used to make steel.

Underground layers of coal are called seams. In the United States, many coal seams are near the Earth's surface. Strip mining is used to remove this coal. In strip mining, huge mechanical shovels and bulldozers strip the vegetation and soil from the land above the coal. Then, machines dig out the coal. Where there are deeper coal deposits, miners dig long tunnels down to the coal seams. Miners work deep down in these tunnels to remove the coal.

Americans once used much more coal than they do today. Your grandparents may have heated their homes with coal. Most homes today are heated with oil or natural gas. We still burn coal to make electricity, but burning coal causes high levels of air pollution. Pollution-control devices must be used to remove air pollution from the smokestacks of coal-burning energy plants.

GO ON TO THE NEXT PAGE ☞

87

Coal, p. 2

 **Answer these questions.**

1. Some types of coal contain a lot of sulfur. Burning this coal puts sulfur dioxide into the air. Rain washes sulfur dioxide out of the air and creates a kind of pollution called acid rain. Which type of coal would cause most of this pollution? Why would this be a problem for coal producers in the United States?

_____

_____

_____

2. Why is anthracite coal the best type of coal for fuel?

_____

_____

_____

3. How does strip mining destroy the land?

_____

_____

_____

4. Supplies of all fossil fuels are being used up. What effect might that have on the way we make and use energy?

_____

_____

_____

_____

_____

Water Machines

Moving water can move things. It can make things turn. Many mechanical devices have been invented that make use of the energy of moving water. In early times, grains were ground into flour at a mill. These mills were located by a river. The moving water pushed against the blades of a large water wheel. The wheel turned a large grinding stone inside the mill.

Moving water is also used to produce electricity. A turbine is a modern type of water wheel. The blades of the turbine are turned by moving water. The generator, which is connected to the turbine, produces electric current that is supplied to the consumer. Construct a water wheel as shown.

You will need

★ a nail   ★ a plastic film can   ★ 4 plastic spoons

1. Punch a long nail through the cap and the bottom of a plastic film can. Make four cuts 1 cm wide in the sides. The cuts should be equal distances apart.

2. Cut off half the handle of each of the plastic spoons. Push the shortened handle end of each spoon into each of the four cuts. All of the bowls of the spoons must be facing the same way.

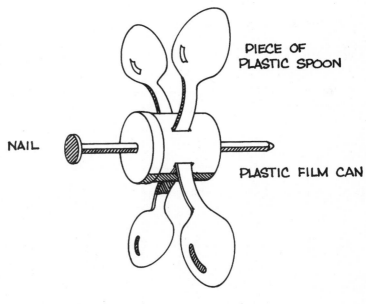

PIECE OF PLASTIC SPOON

NAIL

PLASTIC FILM CAN

3. Hold the water wheel loosely by the ends of the nail. It should turn rapidly if you hold it under a stream of running water from a faucet. Try your water wheel in a bathtub where the water is moving toward the drain.

 Answer these questions on another sheet of paper.

1. How could this water wheel be made to lift a small weight?
2. How is this water wheel like a windmill?
3. What simple machine is part of the water wheel?

Wind Energy

People have used wind energy for a long time to help them do work. Windmills in Europe and in America were used to pump water, grind grain, and saw wood. Later in history, they were also used to generate electricity. Windmills are still used today. Most windmills are found in flat, open country where it is windy.

Today, people are looking for different ways to generate electricity without using fuels. New kinds of wind-powered generators are being tested. The drawing shows one kind of modern windmill. This space-age windmill can generate a great deal of electricity.

Complete the following crossword puzzle.

ACROSS

1. We use the _____ of the wind.

2. Windmills can _____ electricity.

4. Windmills can pump _____.

5. Windmills can _____ corn.

6. Moving air is called _____.

DOWN

1. Windmills can generate _____ energy.

3. Wind energy is used in Europe, Asia, Africa, and _____.

Windmills Old and New

Windmills are machines that use wind power. They are usually used to provide power to pump water or generate electricity. Most windmills have a wheel of blades that is turned by the wind. The shaft of the wheel is mounted on a tower. The shaft is connected to a system of gears that carry power to a water pump or electric generator.

The first windmills were probably invented in the seventh century in Iran. They were used to grind grain. By the twelfth century, windmills were being used in Europe. The Dutch windmills were mainly used to pump water from the land.

Recently, there has been a renewed interest in windmills. This is because wind, unlike fossil fuels, is a renewable source of energy. Modern windmills are much more efficient than the old European windmills. One type of modern windmill is the Darrieus type, which looks like a giant eggbeater. It is up to eight times more efficient than the Dutch windmills. You can make a model of a Darrieus-type windmill.

You will need

- ☆ cardboard tube from a roll of paper towels
- ☆ 2 pieces of tagboard (24 cm long x 7 cm wide)
- ☆ string   ☆ stapler   ☆ hole punch

1. Cut 2 tagboard rotors 24 cm long and 7 cm wide as shown.

2. Punch 2 holes at one end of the tube. Loop a string through the holes and knot it, so the tube hangs from one string.

3. Staple the rotors to the tube, so they flare out, as shown.

4. In a paragraph, tell how effective your model was. What would you do to improve the design?

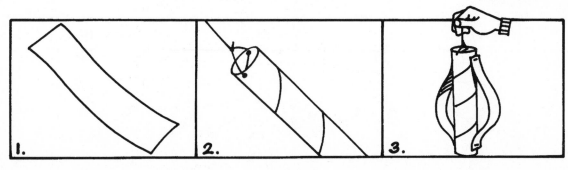

Earth's Atmosphere

We live on the crust of the Earth. We have food and water. But another part of the Earth's structure is needed to keep us alive. That part is called the **atmosphere**. The atmosphere is about 500 miles (800 km) high, and it is held in place by the Earth's gravity. The atmosphere has four layers.

Closest to the Earth is the troposphere, the layer in which we live. The troposphere is only a thin band of the atmosphere, about five to ten miles (8–16 km) thick. All the Earth's weather occurs in the troposphere. The troposphere also contains the air we need to live.

Above the troposphere is the stratosphere, a layer that is from about five to 50 miles (8–80 km) high. The stratosphere has only a few clouds. These clouds are mostly made of ice crystals. In the stratosphere are the fast-moving winds known as the jet stream.

Above the stratosphere is the ionosphere, which stretches from about 50 miles to about 300 miles (80–500 km) above the Earth. There is almost no air in the ionosphere.

The top layer of the atmosphere is called the exosphere. It begins about 300 miles (500 km) above the Earth, but it has no real top boundary. This layer is the beginning of what we call outer space.

 Label the layers of Earth's atmosphere in the picture below. Write *troposphere, stratosphere, ionosphere*, or *exosphere* on the correct line.

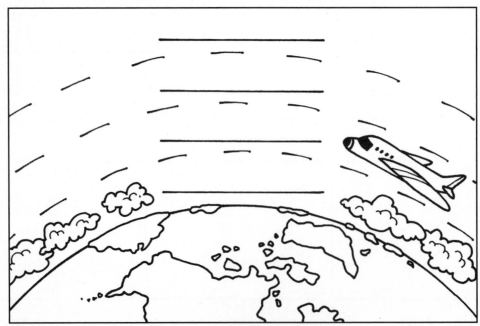

What Is Air Made Of?

You can't see **air**. It is made up of invisible gases. Two of these gases, nitrogen and oxygen, make up almost all of the air. Most living things cannot survive without oxygen. For example, we need oxygen to help our bodies get energy from the food we eat.

Living things need nitrogen to make new cells, but they cannot take the nitrogen directly from the air. Nitrogen must first be combined with other elements. The air contains other gases, too, such as carbon dioxide. We give off carbon dioxide when we breathe out and when we burn fuel. Carbon dioxide and the other gases besides nitrogen and oxygen make up just one part in a hundred parts of air.

COMPOSITION OF AIR

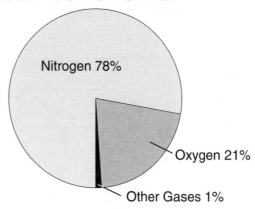

Nitrogen 78%

Oxygen 21%

Other Gases 1%

Answer these questions.

1. How much of the air is made up of nitrogen? _____

2. Which gas makes up 21 percent of the air? _____

3. How much of the air is made up of other gases? _____

4. We breathe in oxygen and give off carbon dioxide. Is there more oxygen or more

carbon dioxide in the air? _____

5. Which gas makes up the largest part of air? _____

The Nitrogen Cycle

Most of the gas in air is nitrogen. Nitrogen is also found in living things. It cycles back and forth between living things and nonliving things. Plants and animals need nitrogen to stay alive and to grow. Most living things, however, cannot take nitrogen directly out of the air. It must first be changed into a nitrogen compound that they can use.

In nature, nitrogen compounds are formed in two ways. Lightning and rain cause some nitrogen molecules from the air to combine with oxygen molecules. Then, the compounds that result, the nitrates, can be found in the soil. These nitrates can be taken in by plants.

Nitrogen compounds are also formed by small living things called nitrogen-fixing bacteria. These tiny living things are able to take nitrogen right out of the air. When plants and animals die, decay bacteria break down their body parts. The nitrogen compounds return to the soil. Living animals also get rid of some nitrogen compounds in their waste materials. Other bacteria break down the nitrogen compounds in the soil. They take the nitrogen out and return it to the air. Then, the **nitrogen cycle** continues.

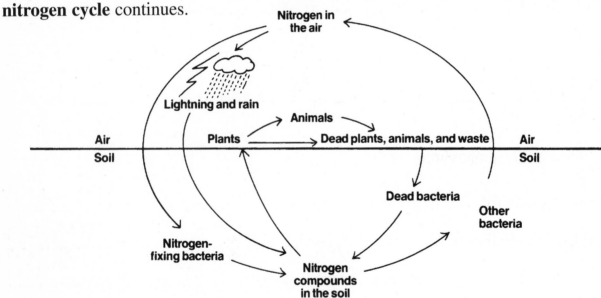

Study the diagram. Answer these questions on another sheet of paper.

1. How are lightning and rain important to the nitrogen cycle?
2. What living things can use nitrogen right from the air?
3. Where do most plants get nitrogen compounds?
4. Where do animals get nitrogen compounds?
5. What do living things use nitrogen compounds for?
6. What happens to the nitrogen in dead plants and animals?
7. Are bacteria very important to the nitrogen cycle?

The Water Cycle

Water often changes from its liquid form to its gaseous form and back to its liquid form in a process called the **water cycle**. The three main steps in the water cycle are evaporation, condensation, and precipitation. Evaporation is necessary to get the liquid water into its gaseous form of water vapor in the air. Condensation is needed to turn the vapor back to a liquid in the clouds. And precipitation returns the liquid water to the Earth.

Evaporation occurs as liquid water is heated and changed into water vapor. The water vapor is then carried up into the sky by rising air. Condensation takes place as the rising water vapor cools and is changed into liquid water, forming clouds. Precipitation happens as water droplets grow heavy and fall to the Earth as rain, snow, or some other type of precipitation.

 **Label the steps of the water cycle in the picture below. Write** *evaporation,* *condensation,* **or** *precipitation* **on the correct line.**

Making Fresh Water

"Water, water, everywhere, and not a drop to drink." Almost all the water on the Earth is in the ocean. And even though ocean water isn't poisonous, if you drink enough of it, you'll die of thirst. Your body will dehydrate, or dry out, as it works to get rid of the extra salt. But wouldn't it be useful if you could separate the salt from the water? Try this activity to find out if you can.

You will need

☆ salt   ☆ clear plastic cup   ☆ very warm tap water
☆ spoon   ☆ small plastic plate   ☆ clear plastic bowl

1. Put one spoonful of salt into the cup.

2. Add very warm water to the cup until it is half full, and stir. The salt should dissolve, or disappear, into the water.

3. Set the cup of water on the plastic plate. Put the clear plastic bowl upside down over the cup of salt water.

4. Check your setup after 15 minutes. If water has collected on the inside of the clear plastic bowl, taste it.

5. With your teacher's permission, take a small sip of the water in the cup. (Drinking a small sip of salt water is not dangerous. Your body won't get any more salt than it would from eating a few crackers.)

6. Record your observations.

◻ **Answer these questions on another sheet of paper.**

1. What did you find after 15 minutes?
2. How did the water inside the bowl taste? How did the water in the cup taste?
3. How can you explain what happened in this activity?
4. What do you think happened to the salt in the cup?
5. In some parts of the world, people get drinking water from desalination plants. Desalination plants separate fresh water from salt water, much as you did in this activity. One problem with desalination plants is that they require large amounts of energy to operate them. What is the energy needed for? Is energy needed in your activity? Explain.
6. Why do you think it is difficult and expensive to obtain large quantities of drinking water from salt water?

Earth's Surfaces and the Temperature

This activity will help you to see that different surfaces on the Earth are heated at different rates by the Sun.

You will need

★ coat hanger   ★ thermometer   ★ Styrofoam cup

1. First bend the coat hanger into a stand as shown in the picture. Then, push the thermometer through a slot you make in the bottom of the Styrofoam cup.

2. Hang the thermometer and cup on the coat hanger stand. Then, take your assembly outside.

3. Measure the air temperature in the following places: a. over blacktop; b. over concrete; c. in the shade of a tree; d. in the shade of a building.

4. Record the temperature at each location. Show all the temperatures in the chart below.

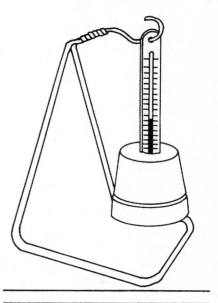

AIR TEMPERATURE

Location of Thermometer	Temperature (°F)
Over Blacktop	
Over Concrete	
In Shade of Tree	
In Shade of Building	

 Answer these questions.

1. Observation: Was the temperature higher in direct sunlight or in the shade?

_____

_____

2. Conclusion: How did the temperature differ over dark and light surfaces?

_____

_____

Cold Air Meets Hot Air

Severe weather often occurs where a cold **air mass** meets a hot air mass. This activity will help you to see what happens when the two air masses meet.

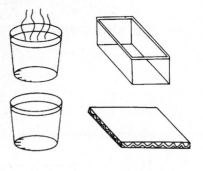

You will need

- ⭐ red and blue food coloring
- ⭐ piece of plastic or cardboard
- ⭐ hot water (Be careful!)
- ⭐ plastic box
- ⭐ cold water

1. Stir red food coloring into some hot water. Stir blue food coloring into some cold water.

2. Use a piece of plastic or cardboard to divide the plastic box into two halves.

3. At the same time, pour the hot water into one half of the box and the cold water into the other half.

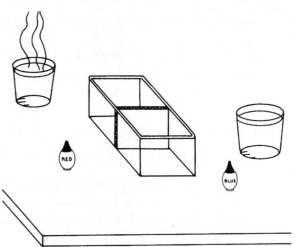

4. Predict what will happen when you lift the divider. Then, slowly lift it. Watch what happens.

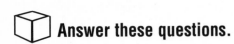 **Answer these questions.**

1. Observation: What did you see when the two kinds of water met?

_____

_____

2. Conclusion: The hot water is like what kind of air mass?

_____

3. Conclusion: The cold water is like what kind of air mass?

_____

4. Conclusion: What kind of front is the model like?

_____

Wind and Surface Features

Air moves from places of high pressure to places of low pressure. The moving air is called **wind**. The speed and direction of wind are affected by the surface features of the land. Tall mountains and deep valleys affect the winds.

A wind vane is a device that shows the direction of wind movement. Try the following activity to make your own wind vane.

You will need

★ soda straw   ★ eraser-tipped pencil   ★ straight pin   ★ feather

1. Push the shaft of the feather into one end of the straw.

2. Find the center of balance on your straw (the point at which it will balance on your finger tip).

3. Push the straight pin through the straw at the center of balance. This will be nearer to the end with the feather than the open end of the straw.

4. Wiggle the pin around so that the straw spins freely.

5. Push the pin into the eraser of the pencil.

The wind vane is now ready to use. Remember that a wind vane points to the direction from which the wind is coming. Draw an outline of your school or home on another sheet of paper. Take your wind vane to several spots around the building. Notice the direction of the wind. Draw an arrow at these spots on your map to indicate the direction from which the wind is coming.

 Answer these questions.

1. Do all of the arrows point the same way? _____

2. What are some things that might cause different wind directions around the

building? _____

_____

_____

What Weather Reaches the Ground?

Scientists can often tell if rain, snow, or sleet will fall from clouds to the ground. It depends on temperature. For example, if falling snow passes through air that has a temperature above the freezing point (0° C), the snow may melt and turn to rain. If raindrops pass through air that has a temperature below the freezing point, the rain may turn to sleet.

 Study the pictures below. Each one shows the temperature of the clouds, the air below the clouds, and the ground. Decide what the weather will probably be. Write *rain, snow,* or *sleet* under each picture.

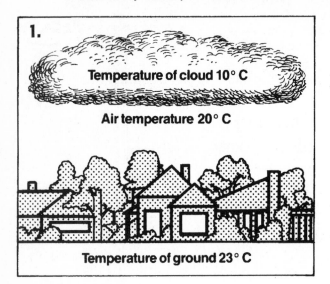

1. Temperature of cloud 10° C
Air temperature 20° C
Temperature of ground 23° C

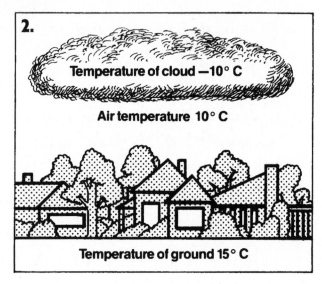

2. Temperature of cloud −10° C
Air temperature 10° C
Temperature of ground 15° C

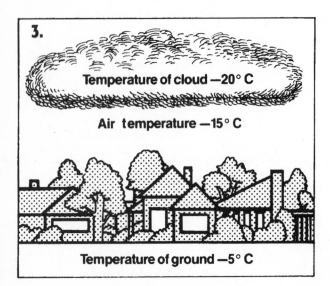

3. Temperature of cloud −20° C
Air temperature −15° C
Temperature of ground −5° C

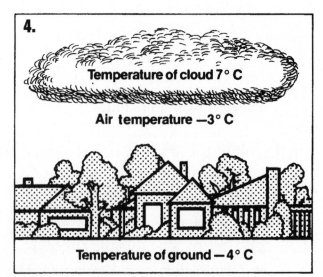

4. Temperature of cloud 7° C
Air temperature −3° C
Temperature of ground −4° C

Cloud Formation

Have you ever watched **clouds** float across the sky? How do the great clouds form? This activity is designed to show you how a cloud forms.

You will need

- ☆ jar
- ☆ plastic wrap
- ☆ hot water
- ☆ tape
- ☆ ice cubes

1. Slowly fill the jar with very hot water.

2. Pour out all but 2.5 cm (1 in.) of the water.

3. Tape a piece of plastic wrap securely over the top of the jar.

4. Place 2 or 3 ice cubes on the plastic wrap. Then, place the jar in sunlight.

5. Observe the inside of the jar.

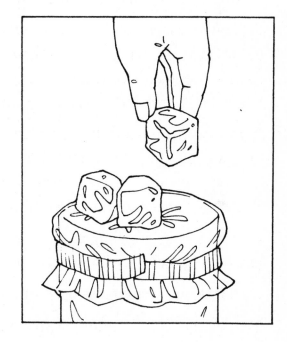

Answer these questions.

1. What did you see inside the jar above the water?

2. The air above the hot water is warm and moist and holds a lot of water vapor. What do you think happens when the warm, moist air rises toward the ice cubes?

3. What happens when warm, moist air is cooled?

4. What forms when tiny droplets of water float in the air?

5. Do you think the temperature is hot or cold where clouds form? Why?

Nature's Weather Clues

You can use plants and animals to help you find out more about the weather. Some plants and animals give warnings, or signs, about coming rain.

1. Daisies, tulips, and morning glories usually close their blossoms before a rain.

2. Clover leaves often fold up before a storm.

3. Butterflies seem to disappear before a rain. They hide to protect their wings.

4. Birds and insects usually fly close to the ground before a rain.

5. Cows will sometimes stand together before a storm.

Some plants and animals give clues about temperature. Read the information below and then draw a plant and animal thermometer. Next to the temperatures, write in the weather warning that each plant or animal gives.

1. When the temperature is above freezing, the leaves of rhododendron plants stick out straight. When the temperature dips below freezing, their leaves begin to fold. The colder it gets, the lower their leaves fold down. If the temperature goes below –6°C, rhododendron leaves fold down straight.

2. In the warmer months, listen for katydids. When the air temperature is above 25°C, these insects chirp, "Kay-tee-did-it." As the temperature drops, the call becomes shorter. Around 21°C they chirp, "Kat-tee-did." At 14°C the call is short, "Kate." When the temperature is below 13°C, the katydid doesn't chirp at all.

3. If you see ants crawling around, the temperature is probably above 12°C. If it is any colder, these insects stay in their nests.

4. Cicadas sing when the temperature is above 28°C.

5. The warmer it is, the more active bees become. There is a limit, though. When the temperature is above 39°C, bees don't go far from their hives.

Watch for these weather clues. See if they can help you predict the weather.

Reading a Weather Chart

You can learn about the climate in a place by reading **weather data**.

 Read the chart below. It shows how much rain and snow usually fall in one year in eight cities in the United States.

City	Yearly Rainfall	Yearly Snowfall
Bakersfield, California	15 cm	0 cm
Caribou, Maine	83 cm	229 cm
Charleston, South Carolina	104 cm	13 cm
Chicago, Illinois	98 cm	131 cm
Dallas, Texas	56 cm	4 cm
Duluth, Minnesota	65 cm	143 cm
Phoenix, Arizona	15 cm	0 cm
Washington, D.C.	74 cm	51 cm

 Answer these questions.

1. Which three cities usually have more snow than rain in one year?

_____

2. Which city usually receives the most snow? _____

3. About how much rain does Charleston usually receive in one year?

_____

4. If you sold umbrellas, which two cities would not be very good places for you to

work? _____

5. If you sold snow shovels, which three cities would be good places to do business?

_____

6. Which cities usually do not receive any snow? _____

7. Would it make sense for somebody to build a ski resort in Dallas? _____

Explain. _____

Weather Symbols

Today's weather forecast for the country is as follows:
There will be showers and thunderstorms along the East Coast from Maine to
Virginia. A high-pressure center is sitting over Texas. Low pressure is moving into
the Pacific Northwest, bringing snow to the Rocky Mountains.

Use the weather symbols shown below to fill in this forecast on the map.

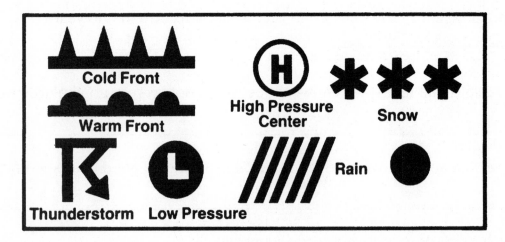

Making Your Own Forecast

 Imagine that you are a television weather reporter. You have to report today's weather. Write your script in the space provided. Use the weather data given in the chart below to help write your weather report. Present your forecast to the class.

WEATHER SUMMARY

Temperature	25° C
Wind	10 mph
Wind direction	SW
Cloud cover	25%, scattered cumulus
Precipitation	0.00 in last 24 hr

Write your weather report here.

_____

_____

_____

_____

_____

_____

_____

_____

_____

_____

_____

How the Solar System Formed

Mercury Venus Earth Mars Jupiter Saturn Uranus Neptune Pluto

There are many theories about how our **solar system** began. According to one, gravitation played a very important part. Some scientists think the solar system was once a huge cloud of whirling gas and dust. Each bit of matter in the cloud had a gravitational pull. Each bit was, therefore, pulled toward others. The bits of matter began to come together. The cloud became smaller and more dense. It flattened into a spinning disk. Temperature and pressure in the center of the disk increased. They became so great that powerful explosions began and our Sun was born.

Huge clouds still whirled in the outer part of the disk. They circled the Sun as it formed. The materials in the clouds began to clump together, or condense. The lightweight gases condensed to form the four large planets Jupiter, Saturn, Uranus, and Neptune. Tiny Pluto may have been formed this way, too. Heavier materials condensed to form the inner planets Mercury, Venus, Earth, and Mars. The leftover gases may have become comets, asteroids, and meteors.

Read each sentence. Write *T* on the line if the sentence is true. Write *F* if the sentence is false.

_____ **1.** Only one theory exists on how the solar system began.

_____ **2.** Our solar system may have started as a huge cloud of gas and dust.

_____ **3.** Each bit of matter in the cloud had a gravitational pull.

_____ **4.** Temperatures and pressures in the cloud resulted in powerful explosions.

_____ **5.** The clouds in the outer part of the disk formed the Sun.

_____ **6.** Jupiter, Saturn, and Mars are all gaseous planets.

_____ **7.** Comets and asteroids may have formed from leftover gases.

Blue Skies, Orange Sunsets

Sunlight is white light. It is made up of all the colors of the rainbow. So, why does the sky look blue? Why does the setting sun look orange? You can make a model to find out.

You will need

★ a clear jar ★ water ★ fat-free milk ★ flashlight ★ a partner

1. Fill the jar with water. Darken the room. Have a partner shine the flashlight through the water. Look at the light coming into the water.

   What color is the light? _____

2. Stir a few drops of milk into the water. Stand on the opposite side of the jar from the flashlight. Look directly at the beam of light as it goes through the water.

   What color is the light? _____

3. Look at the jar from the side. What color is the light coming through the water?

   _____

4. Where does the orange light come from? the blue light?

   _____

   _____

When you look through the water and see orange, the blue light is not reaching your eyes. It is bouncing off the milk particles away from your eyes. You can see the blue color when you look at the beam of light from the side.

The sky is blue for the same reason. When you look at the sky, you are looking at air full of water droplets and bits of dust. The air is like the milky water in the jar. The dust and water scatter the colors in the Sun's light. Blue light is scattered more than the other colors. It bounces to your eyes from all parts of the sky and makes the sky look blue. When you look at the Sun, you see the yellow that has not been scattered but travels straight to Earth from the Sun.

At sunset, the Sun is low in the sky. Its light goes through more bits of dust and drops of water. Even more of the blue and violet light gets scattered. This leaves more reds and yellows to make colorful sunsets.

From the Moon, the sky looks black. Why? (Hint: There is no air on the Moon.)

Meteor Showers

Have you ever heard of a **meteor shower**? A meteor shower occurs when the Earth travels through the orbit of a group of meteoroids. This happens several times each year. During a meteor shower, thousands of meteors streak across the sky. The diagram shows the orbit of one group of meteors. There are really many more. Meteor showers are named for the group of stars that are located in the same part of the sky. The chart shows ten meteor showers that occur each year.

Name	Date	Number per hour
Quadrantids	January 3	30
Lyrids	April 23	8
Eta Aquarids	May 4	10
Delta Aquarids	July 30	15
Perseids	August 12	40
Orionids	October 21	15
Taurids	November 4	8
Leonids	November 16	6
Geminids	December 13	50
Ursids	December 22	12

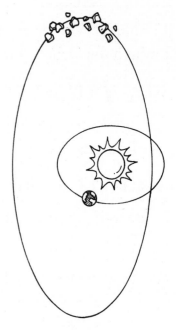

Answer these questions.

1. Which two meteor showers would give you the best show in the evening sky?

_____

2. Which meteor shower takes place around the time of the winter solstice?

_____

3. When are the meteors that are seen close to Orion visible?

_____

4. How many meteors can be seen in the Orionids meteor shower?

_____

5. Why can the time of a meteor shower be predicted?

_____

Famous Comets

Many **comets** are named for the people who first saw them. Read the chart below. It shows when some famous comets were last seen. It also shows how long it takes for each comet to make a complete orbit.

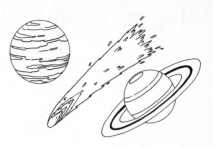

Name of Comet	Year Last Seen	Orbit Length in Years	Year Next Seen
Great Comet of 1811	1811	3,000	
Olber's Comet	1963	74	
Great Comet of 1843	1843	513	
Great Comet of 1882	1882	760	
Comet Humason	1961	2,900	
Comet Tago-Sato-Kosaka	1969	420,000	
Comet Bennett	1969	1,680	
Comet Kohoutek	1973	75,000	

Figure out when each comet may be seen again. Add the length of each comet's orbit to the date it was last seen. Write the answers on the lines.

1. Which comet might you be able to see in your lifetime?

_____

2. Which comet has the shortest orbit length in years? When will it be visible again?

_____

_____

3. Which comet has the longest orbit length in years? How long is its orbit length?

_____

_____

4. If you were to discover a comet, what would you name it?

_____

The Phases of the Moon

As the Moon travels around the Earth, it looks as if it is changing shape. These changing shapes are called the **phases of the Moon**.

Read each description of a phase of the Moon. Then, draw a picture of the Moon that shows that phase.

1. When the side of the Moon facing the Earth is dark, it is a New Moon.

2. A few days after the New Moon, you can see a small, curved part of the Moon shaped like a crescent. The lighted crescent appears to be on the right.

3. Seven days after a New Moon, you can see a Half Moon. The lighted half appears on the right.

4. Soon, you can see three quarters of the Moon. This phase is called the Gibbous Moon. The lighted section is on the right.

5. Two weeks after the New Moon, you can see the entire lighted side of the Moon. This is the Full Moon.

6. A few days later, you can see three quarters of the lighted surface. However, the lighted part is on the left this time. This is also a Gibbous Moon.

7. Seven days after a Full Moon, you can see another Half Moon. However, the left half is lighted this time.

8. Finally, another Crescent Moon is visible. However, this time the lighted crescent is on the left.

How Far Is the Moon?

You are learning about the Earth's satellite, the Moon. In this activity, you will find the distance between the Earth and the Moon.

You will need

☆ index card   ☆ string 2 m (80 in.) long   ☆ tape
☆ metric ruler   ☆ scissors

1. As shown in the picture, cut a round notch in one edge of the index card. The notch should be exactly 1 cm (2.5 in.) wide.

2. On a night when there is a Full Moon, tape the card to a window from which you can see the Moon. Then, tape one end of the string to the card.

3. Look at the Moon through the notch in the card. As you hold the end of the string, back up until the Moon fills the notch.

4. Carefully hold the string up to your eye. Have another person measure the length of the string between the notch and your eye.

5. Multiply the length of the string by 3,500 km (2,170 mi.). This will tell you the distance.

 Answer these questions.

1. What was the length of the string? _____

2. What is the distance from the Earth to the Moon? _____

How Long Is a Year?

A **year** is based on how long a planet takes to orbit the Sun. Each planet's year has a different length.

The graph below shows the length of the years for the planets measured in Earth years. Use it to answer the questions.

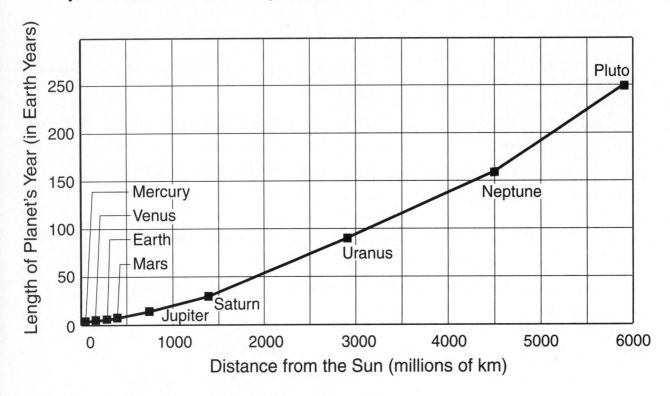

1. What do the numbers across the bottom of the graph show?

   _____

2. What do the numbers along the side of the graph show?

   _____

3. What does the slope of the line on the graph show?

   _____

4. Which planet has the longest year? _____

5. How far is Neptune from the Sun? _____

6. How long is a year on Saturn? _____

The Pull of the Planets

The planets are different sizes. Some are larger than Earth. Some are smaller. Their **gravitational pulls** are different, too. If you could go to the planets, you would have a different weight on each one. On Mercury, for example, the gravitational pull is 28 percent of that on Earth. So, on Mercury your weight would be only about one fourth your Earth weight. To find out exactly how weight changes, try this.

Suppose a baby weighs 5 kilograms. What would the baby weigh on Mercury?

1. Mercury has a surface gravity of 28%.

2. Change 28% to 0.28.

3. Multiply 5 kilograms x 0.28 = 1.40 kilograms.

Find out how much this baby would weigh on the other planets. Use the information in the chart to help you. The first one has been done for you.

Planet	Surface gravity compared with Earth	Weight of child who weighs 5 kilograms on Earth
Mercury	28%	1.40 kg
Venus	85%	
Mars	38%	
Jupiter	260%	
Saturn	120%	
Uranus	110%	
Neptune	140%	

The surface gravity of Pluto is not known.

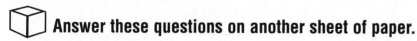 **Answer these questions on another sheet of paper.**

1. On which planet would you probably weigh the least?
2. On which planet would you weigh the most?
3. On which planets would you weigh more than you weigh on Earth?
4. On which planets would you weigh less than you weigh on Earth?
5. Why is there a difference in gravity of the planets?

The Moon, Comets, and Meteors

📦 **Read each statement below. If it is true about the Moon, write *Moon* on the line. If it is true about comets, write *comet*. If it is true about meteors, write *meteor*. Some of the statements are true for more than one thing.**

_____ **1.** It always follows the same path around the Earth.

_____ **2.** When it is near the Sun, sunlight makes it look as though it is glowing.

_____ **3.** Because of friction with air, its gases get hot enough to glow.

_____ **4.** It is a space rock that starts falling toward the Earth.

_____ **5.** "Dirty snowball" is its nickname.

_____ **6.** It gives off no light of its own.

_____ **7.** It seems to change shape during each month.

_____ **8.** It follows an orbit in space.

_____ **9.** It is part of the solar system.

_____ **10.** "Shooting star" is its nickname.

_____ **11.** Its streak of light usually lasts for only a few seconds.

_____ **12.** When it blocks the light of the Sun, it causes an eclipse.

_____ **13.** Every time it orbits the Sun, it becomes smaller.

Solar Eclipses

An eclipse of the Sun is called a **solar eclipse**. During a solar eclipse, the Moon moves directly between the Earth and the Sun. The Moon shuts out the view of the Sun. The shadow of the Moon falls on the Earth.

A solar eclipse starts when the Moon begins to pass in front of the Sun. At first, it blocks only a small part of the Sun from view. Soon, almost the entire surface of the Sun is hidden. (This is called a total eclipse.) The daytime sky darkens. For a few minutes it seems as if it is late evening. Then, more and more of the Sun becomes visible as the Moon continues to move. The eclipse ends when the Moon no longer blocks the Sun.

Scientists can learn a lot about the Sun during a solar eclipse. However, a total eclipse cannot be seen from any one spot for longer than 7 minutes and 40 seconds. That doesn't give the scientists much time to make their observations. So, during a solar eclipse in 1973, a group of scientists took their equipment aboard a jet. The jet sped across the sky, all the time staying in the Moon's narrow shadow. These scientists were able to study a total eclipse for 74 minutes.

Answer these questions.

1. What is a solar eclipse? _____

_____

2. What causes a solar eclipse? _____

_____

3. How long can a total eclipse be seen from one place? _____

_____

The Moon in an Eclipse

 Draw the position of the Moon during a total solar eclipse. Show the shadows.

1. From where on Earth would a solar eclipse be visible? _____

_____

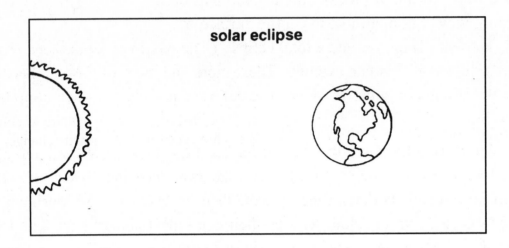

solar eclipse

 Draw the position of the Moon during a lunar eclipse. Show the shadows.

2. From where on Earth would a lunar eclipse be visible? _____

_____

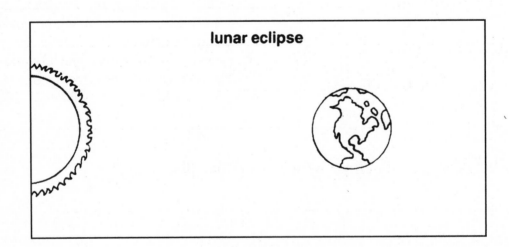

lunar eclipse

Unit 3: Life Science

BACKGROUND INFORMATION

Living and Nonliving Things

All living things carry on activities that nonliving things do not. These life processes define a living thing. All living things grow, or increase in size and the amount of matter they contain. All living things can reproduce, or make more of the same kind of organism. Living things consume energy, change it, and excrete, or give off, waste. Living things react to stimuli and to changes in the environment.

Living things are made up of cells. A cell is the smallest living unit. It has all of the properties of a living thing. Most cells contain a nucleus, cytoplasm, and a cell membrane. Plant cells have, in addition, a cell wall, which is outside of the membrane. The cell wall makes the plant cell stiffer than the animal cell. The growth of a living thing is caused by the growth and division of its cells. Single-celled organisms are called microorganisms.

Nonliving things may carry on some of these activities, but because they do not carry on all of these activities, they are not living. Students may be confused about what is living and what is not. Water seems to move, change, and appear alive. A flame will flicker and grow. Even scientists disagree about certain things, such as viruses. Distinguishing between living and nonliving things can be difficult, but students can follow the guidelines above to grasp the concept.

The Biosphere

The biosphere includes the atmosphere, the upper surface of the Earth's crust, and the oceans. The Sun can also be considered part of the biosphere, as its energy is used by living things. Life on Earth is contained in the biosphere. Here, living things grow, reproduce, and die. In the process they interact with each other, with nonliving things, and with their environment. They

change to adapt to their environments, and they change their environments. Any study of the biosphere includes the study of the relationships between the plants and animals that live there. The interactions between the plants and animals in the biosphere consist of energy chains, or food chains.

The Web of Life: Life Cycles, Communities, and Food Chains

All living things go through life cycles. From single-celled organisms to the largest animals, these life cycles include growth, change, consumption of food and water, use of energy, reproduction, and death. Reproduction varies among life forms. Plants reproduce by seeds or spores. Animals may lay eggs or give birth to live young. Some offspring resemble the parents and others do not. Some animals, such as frogs, undergo metamorphosis, or a complete change, during their lifetimes. The successful reproduction of a species is important to the population's continued growth or stability.

Populations are plants or animals of one kind that live in one area. Scientists are interested in keeping track of population numbers so that they can tell if a population is in danger of extinction. Populations are estimated by counting the population in several different sample areas and finding an average. Moving populations, such as animals, are more difficult to count.

Populations interact to form communities. Each community may have many different habitats. Each population has its own habitat. The interactions of populations in a community create food chains. These interdependencies are known as symbiosis, or living together in close association.

A typical food chain begins with plants. Most plants make their own food. Algae make their food from nonliving things. Plant cells have chloroplasts, which trap energy from the Sun. Water and carbon dioxide enter the cell through the cell wall. The cell turns the water and gas into food and oxygen. The cell uses the food and passes off the oxygen to be used by other living things. Plants also produce sugar and starch, which are used by other animals. The animals that use plants are herbivores (plant eaters), carnivores (meat eaters who eat the plant eaters), and omnivores (plant and animal eaters). The animals give off carbon dioxide, which is used by the plants. Food webs are used to describe overlapping food chains. These communities and the interactions within them are complex. When their natural order is disrupted, the balance of nature is affected, and organisms can be in danger. The most dire consequence of this disruption is the extinction of a species.

The relationships between organisms in a community can be described in three ways. If the relationship between two organisms is beneficial to both, it is called mutualism. If the relationship helps one organism while the other is neither helped nor harmed, it is called commensalism. If the relationship helps one organism and harms the other, it is known as parasitism.

A community contains food makers, or producers; food takers, or consumers; and decomposers. Typically, the producers are plants. Both other plants and animals eat plants. Carnivores also need plants, as they live off the animals that eat plants. Consumers eat plants, animals, or plants and animals. An animal that eats another animal is a predator. The animal that is eaten is the prey. When the producers and the consumers die, they begin to change; they rot and decay. The decomposers get their food from wastes and dead organisms. Molds, yeast, and bacteria break down the dead matter and give off carbon dioxide. The carbon dioxide is then used by green plants to make food.

The Human Factor

Organisms need to adapt to and change with the changes in their environment to survive. Organisms adapt through physical changes that help them live in their particular habitats and through habits, such as migration, that help them survive. Although many events can disrupt a community and its balance, humans have had the greatest impact upon the Earth's environment. Humans need not only food and energy but also power and space for settlement. Humans create wastes that are not natural to the environment. This environmental pollution is an important concern for everyone. If it is not controlled, the balance of nature is disrupted, organisms die, and those that depend upon the dead organisms may die. It is crucial for humans to find ways to live without creating such disturbances in the environment.

Plant Classification

The plant kingdom contains about 450,000 different kinds of plants, which are each classified into several divisions. The four main classifications for plants are: algae (almost all live in water; from microscopic single-celled plants to seaweed); bryophyta (mosses and liverworts; live in moist places; produce spores); pteridophyta (ferns, clubmosses, horsetails; no flowers); and permatophyta (largest group, with over 350,000 species; reproduce by way of seeds).

Flowering plants are the most numerous type of plant on Earth. They are further classified into groups. Some of the common groups of flowering plants are: grass family (corn, barley, rice, wheat); lily family (violets, hyacinths, tulips, onions, asparagus); palm family (coconut, date); rose family (strawberries, peaches, cherries, apples, and other fruits); legume family (peas, beans, peanuts); beech family; and composite family (sunflowers and others with flowers that are actually many small flowers).

Photosynthesis

Most plants are green. The reason that green plants are green is because they contain chlorophyll, most of which is in the leaves. Chlorophyll is contained in small structures in the leaves called chloroplasts. There are some plants that contain chlorophyll but whose leaves are not green. This is because the chlorophyll has been masked by other pigmentation in the plant. Chlorophyll is necessary for the making of food, but the chlorophyll itself is not used in the food that is made.

Photosynthesis depends on light. A plant that is deprived of light loses its chlorophyll (and its ability to make food) and eventually will die. Plants take in the energy from the Sun and carbon, oxygen, and hydrogen from the air and water. Water and nutrients enter a plant through its roots. Carbon dioxide enters a plant through tiny holes (stomata) in the bottoms of leaves. The plants change these raw materials into carbohydrates and oxygen. The carbohydrates (in the form of a simple sugar called glucose, and starch) are used and stored in the plants for food. The oxygen is released into the air and water where the plants live. In this way, plants constantly replenish the Earth's oxygen supply. Animals breathe the oxygen that plants supply. Animals also supply the carbon dioxide that plants need to survive. This is the oxygen-carbon dioxide cycle.

Green plants are the producers of a community. They not only produce their own food but also are the essential source of food and energy for all communities.

Movement

When animal populations move, it is called migration. When plant populations move, it is called succession. Plants move for different reasons than animals. If vegetation in a particular area is destroyed, seeds will eventually move into the area. New life begins to grow. Grasses and small plants arrive first, then the pines, and finally hardwood trees.

Animal Classification

The animal kingdom can be classified into two large groups: the vertebrates (those with backbones) and the invertebrates (those without backbones). The backbone supports the body and provides flexibility. The spinal cord extends from the brain through the backbone, or spine. Individual nerves branch out from the spinal cord to different parts of the body. Messages from the brain are sent throughout the body through the spinal cord.

Some animals without backbones are sponges, jellyfish, clams, worms, insects, and spiders. Some of these animals have networks of nerves throughout their bodies with no central nerve cords. Many, like insects, have hard exoskeletons that protect their bodies and give them shape.

Animals Are Suited to Their Environments

Animals live in almost every type of environment on Earth. Each kind of animal has become well suited to its environment through generations of adaptation. Those animals that are not suited to the environment, or that are poorly adapted, do not survive. The animals that are most fit for their environments continue to reproduce and make others like themselves. Most animals are suited to either land or water life. An obvious adaptation for fish is the gills that allow them to breathe in the water. Lungs allow land animals to breathe in air.

Every part of an animal helps it to live in its particular environment. Some animals are colored in ways that help them to blend in to their environments. They are camouflaged to protect them from their enemies. Other animals are brightly colored to attract mates and help them with the continuation of their species. Animals' mouths and teeth are adapted to the types of food that they eat. Meat-eating animals have sharp teeth for tearing and ripping their prey, and other teeth for chewing the meat. Animals that eat leaves and grasses have large flat teeth for chewing.

Adaptations to Environment

Animals are adapted to their environments through structures and behaviors. The structures include the physical makeup of animals, some of which were mentioned in the previous section. The behaviors of animals include things like migration and hibernation. In winter, many birds migrate to warmer climates in the south. Some animals, like moose and caribou, also have migratory routes. Many animals hibernate, or sleep, through the winter months. They work through the fall to store food in their bodies that carries them through the winter months. While they sleep, their body processes slow.

Reproduction

All living things have a life cycle within which they take in food and gases, metabolize, excrete waste, reproduce, and die. If living things fail to reproduce or to create healthy offspring, their species will die out.

Animals reproduce in different ways. Some lay eggs, and others give birth to live young. Some offspring look like their parents while others do not. Most reptiles, amphibians, fish, and insects lay eggs. The young of many of these animals can move about and find food for themselves soon after they hatch. Birds also lay eggs, but the adult birds remain with the eggs and care for the young until they can find their own food. Most mammals bear live young. The young are fed milk from the body. Mammals spend more time than other animals feeding, protecting, and teaching their young to survive on their own. Animals that give birth to live young have fewer offspring than those that do not tend to their young. The young of human beings require more care from their parents than any other animal.

The life cycles of some animals include a metamorphosis. A metamorphosis is a complete change in the appearance of an animal. The most striking metamorphosis is the change from caterpillar to butterfly.

Health

Health for children revolves around healthy foods, plenty of exercise, and good hygiene. As children grow, they should begin to recognize that they can make choices that will help them live healthy lives. They need to learn the connections between what they eat and the way they look and feel. They need to have the basic information that will help them to make good food choices. Children need to know that it is never too early to begin healthy habits in eating, exercise, and hygiene. The habits they form now will affect their lives for many years to come.

Nutrition

The body needs to receive certain nutrients in order to grow and to stay healthy. These nutrients are broken down into six types: carbohydrates, protein, fat, vitamins, minerals, and water.

- Carbohydrates are sugars and starches. Sugars, such as fruits and honey, give the body quick energy while the starches, such as bread, cereal, and rice, give the body stored energy.

- Proteins come from foods such as milk, cheese, lean meat, fish, peas, and beans. They help the body to repair itself. Proteins are used by the body to build muscle and bone, and they give the body energy.

- Fat is important for energy, too, and it helps to keep the body warm, but if the body does not use the fats put into it, it will store the fat. Fats come from foods such as meat, milk, butter, oil, and nuts.

- Vitamins are important to the body in many ways. Vitamins help the other nutrients in a person's body work together. Lack of certain vitamins can cause serious illnesses. Vitamin A, for example, which comes from foods such as broccoli, carrots, radishes, and liver, helps with eyesight. Vitamin B from green leafy vegetables, eggs, and milk, helps with growth and energy. Vitamin C from citrus fruits, cauliflower, strawberries, tomatoes, peppers, and broccoli, prevents sickness.

- Milk, vegetables, liver, seafood, and raisins are some of the foods that provide the minerals necessary for growth. Calcium is a mineral that helps with strong bones, and iron is needed for healthy red blood.

- Water makes up most of the human body and helps to keep our temperature normal. It is healthy and recommended to drink several glasses of water each day.

Foods have long been divided into four basic food groups: meat, milk, vegetable-fruit, and bread-cereal. New discoveries have led to a change in the divisions so that in a food pyramid, fruits and vegetables are separated, and fats are included at the top of the pyramid. The recommended servings for each group have also changed over time. Eating the right amount of foods from each group each day gives one a balanced diet. Eating too many foods from one group or not enough of another can lead to deficiencies or weight problems. Although vitamin supplements can help with these deficiencies, vitamins are best absorbed in the body naturally through the digestion of the foods that contain them.

- The Bread-Cereal (Grain) Group contains foods made from grains such as wheat, corn, rice, oats, and barley. Six to eleven servings from this group each day give you carbohydrates, vitamins, and minerals.

- The Vegetable and Fruit Groups contain vitamins, minerals, and carbohydrates. Two to four servings of fruits and three to five servings of vegetables each day are recommended.

- The Meat Group includes chicken, fish, red meats, peas, nuts, and eggs. The meat group contains much of the protein we get from our diets, but it also includes fats. Two to three servings from the meat group each day are recommended.

- The Milk Group includes milk (whole and skim), butter, cheese, yogurt, and ice cream and gives us fat, vitamins, protein and minerals that are important for strong bones and teeth, such as vitamin D. Two to three servings from the milk group each day are recommended.

- The Fats, Oils, and Sweets Group, including butter, oil, and margarine, should be used sparingly.

Hygiene

Keeping the body clean is an important part of staying healthy. Children need to know that when they wash, they are washing off viruses and bacteria, or germs, which can cause illness. Washing the hair and body regularly prevents bacteria from entering the skin through cuts and from getting into the mouth. Hands should always be washed after handling garbage or using the bathroom. Germs can also come from other people. Children should be discouraged from sharing straws, cups, or other utensils. They should be reminded to always cover their mouths when they sneeze or cough, and to use tissues frequently. Children also need to be reminded not to share combs or hats.

Teeth

Regular brushing and flossing can help keep teeth healthy. Avoiding sweets will also help. Most children have all their baby teeth by the time they are two years old. When they are about seven, they will begin to lose their baby teeth, and permanent teeth will begin to appear. Although the baby teeth will fall out, it is important to take good care of them and the gums that surround them.

Decay is caused by acids in the mouth that eat the enamel. The acids are caused by bacteria that live on the food in your mouth. If you brush and floss regularly, the food is taken out of your mouth, and the bacteria cannot live there. When you brush, you remove the plaque from your teeth, as well. Plaque is the sticky yellow film that develops on your teeth from food, bacteria, and acid. Decay can cause a hole in the tooth called a cavity. It can also harm the gums and cause gum disease. Regular dental exams and X-rays will detect any decay that you may have missed.

Exercise and Sleep

There are over 600 muscles in the human body. Muscles are bundles of tissue that respond to nerve impulses by expanding and contracting. When they expand and contract, they make the blood circulate, move food, expand and contract the chest for breathing, and move the outer parts of the body. Muscles grow when they are used and contract when they are not used. Muscles that become unaccustomed to exercise can be injured by sudden or strenuous activity. This is why muscles should be exercised regularly and in moderation. Exercising the muscles makes the body grow larger and stronger and helps make the heart strong.

Regular exercise can relax the body and help people get a good night's rest. Sleep is an important part of keeping the body healthy. People need different amounts of sleep at different times of their lives. Babies sleep most of the time because their bodies are growing very quickly. School children usually require from eight to ten hours of sleep, and adults need about seven or eight hours. Sleep allows the body and mind to rest.

Health and the Environment

Today, more than ever, people must be aware of the effect of the environment on their health. Pollutants in the air and water, excessive exposure to the Sun or cold, a high pollen count in the air, and breathing in second-hand smoke are examples of environmental hazards. Some of these are more easily within our control, such as being sure to wear sunscreen when outdoors and avoiding prolonged exposure to the sun. Students can have an effect on their own environment when they pick up trash and show respect for their surroundings. Our air and water are necessary to all life on Earth, and students should recognize the importance of keeping them clean.

The environment also presents some natural problems, such as insects that bite and sting, and poisonous plants. Besides causing you pain and irritation, mosquitoes can carry organisms that cause diseases from one person to the next. Ticks can cause Lyme disease. Poisonous plants such as poison ivy, poison oak, and poison sumac should also be avoided. Students should look them up and be able to recognize these plants. All three can cause painful, itchy rashes that can last for weeks.

RELATED READING

- *Animals by Habitat Series* (Raintree Steck-Vaughn, 1997).

- *Biomes Series* (Raintree Steck-Vaughn, 2002).

- *Claws, Coats, and Camouflage: The Ways Animals Fit into Their World* by Susan E. Goodman (Millbrook Press, 2001).

- *Coyote and Badger: Desert Hunters of the Southwest* by Bruce Hiscock (Boyds Mills Press, 2001).

- *A Desert Scrapbook* by Virginia Wright-Frierson (Simon & Schuster, 1996).

- *Food Chains* by Teresa Greenaway (*Cycles in Nature Series*, Raintree Steck-Vaughn, 2001).

- *My Season with Penguins: An Antarctic Journey* by Sophie Webb (Houghton Mifflin, 2000).

- *Once a Wolf: How Wildlife Biologists Fought to Bring Back the Gray Wolf* by Stephen R. Swinburne (Houghton Mifflin, 1999).

- *Salamander Rain: A Lake and Pond Journal* by Kristin Joy Pratt-Serafini (Dawn Publications, 2001).

- *Welcome to the River of Grass* by Jane Yolen (Putnam's, 2001).

- *Wildflowers Around the Year* by Hope Ryden (Clarion Books, 2001).

- *World Habitats Series* (Raintree Steck-Vaughn, 1998).

Unit 3 Assessment

📦 **Choose words from the box to complete the paragraphs.**

water	carnivores	energy	reproduce	food	populations
omnivores	biosphere	living	nonliving	producers	consumers
	decomposers	environment	herbivores	depend	

The atmosphere, the oceans, the Earth's crust, and all the living

things there make up the Earth's 1) _____. The

2) _____ things, such as animals and plants, interact with

the 3) _____ things, such as soil and rocks. All living

things need 4) _____, 5) _____,

and 6) _____. Nonliving things do not

7) _____, or make more organisms like themselves.

A community is made up of 8) _____,

such as green plants, 9) _____, such as animals, and

10) _____, such as molds. Consumers that eat only

plants are called 11) _____. Those that eat only meat

are called 12) _____. Those that eat both meat and plants

are called 13) _____.

Communities are home to many different 14) _____

of animals and plants. They all 15) _____ on each other.

Humans need to take care of the 16) _____. We need to

remember that everything we do affects the world around us.

GO ON TO THE NEXT PAGE 👉

Unit 3 Assessment, p. 2

Answer each question about health.

17. How does a food pyramid help you to eat a healthy diet?

_____

_____

18. Why is it important to know how to read the nutrition information on food labels?

_____

_____

19. What are two reasons that some people are vegetarians?

_____

_____

20. What are three things you can do to keep your teeth healthy?

_____

_____

21. What does exercise do for muscles?

_____

_____

22. Why is it important to be able to recognize dangerous plants?

_____

_____

23. What is good first aid for a cut?

_____

_____

24. How do beaches become polluted?

_____

_____

Living Things

Living things reproduce, or make more organisms like themselves. Living things grow and change. Living things need food and water. Living things need energy.

Decide if each item in the box is a living or nonliving thing. Place each in the correct column.

robot	orange juice	duck	rock
cut flower	pencil	moss	ant

Living Things   **Nonliving Things**

_____   _____

_____   _____

_____   _____

_____   _____

 Answer these questions on another sheet of paper.

1. What are four features of living things?
2. A fungus is on a rotting orange. Is the fungus alive?
3. Imagine there is life somewhere else in the universe. Do you think it will have the same features that life on Earth needs to stay alive?

The Biosphere

Life on Earth is contained in the **biosphere**. The biosphere includes the atmosphere, the oceans, and the crust of the Earth.

Make a drawing of the biosphere. Label each part. You may include the Sun, because the Sun's energy is important to the biosphere.

Answer these questions on another sheet of paper.

1. What would happen to the biosphere if the Earth lost its atmosphere?
2. What are three things that the biosphere needs?
3. Give an example of a life-form that would be found in each of these areas:
   a. the soil   **b.** the ocean   **c.** the air

Name _____ Date _____

Creating a Biosphere

You can create your own biosphere. Here's how.

You will need

- ★ a plastic shoe box or an aquarium with a screen cover
- ★ pebbles   ★ soil   ★ a small plant
- ★ grass seed   ★ water   ★ a cricket

1. Place a layer of pebbles in the shoe box or aquarium.
2. Add a layer of soil, about 1.5 in. (4 cm) thick.
3. Put a small plant in the soil.
4. Sprinkle some grass seed on the soil.
5. Dampen the soil with a small amount of water.
6. Put the cricket in the box.
7. Put the cover on the box.

Answer these questions about your biosphere.

1. What are the living things in your biosphere?

_____

2. What are the nonliving things in your biosphere?

_____

3. Make a list of other living and nonliving things that could be added to your model of the biosphere.

_____

_____

_____

4. What does your biosphere need to stay alive?

_____

_____

5. What could harm your biosphere?

_____

_____

Animals in Their Environments

Animals have special body parts to help them live in their **environments**. These body parts would not help them in a different environment.

Look at the pictures below. In each set, the first picture shows an animal in its own environment. The second picture shows the same animal in a different environment. Decide why the animals couldn't live in the different environment. Write the reason on the lines.

1.

The polar bear has fur.   _____

_____

2.

The fish has gills.   _____

_____

3.

The moose has legs.   _____

_____

Name _____ Date _____

Creating a Habitat

An animal's home is its **habitat**. You can create a habitat for an animal. Here's how.

You will need

- ☆ a 2-liter clear plastic container
- ☆ seeds (grass, radish, wheat)
- ☆ potting soil
- ☆ water
- ☆ 3 or 4 earthworms
- ☆ some black paper

1. Fill the container about one third full with soil.
2. Spread the seeds on the soil, and water the seeds and the soil.
3. Put the earthworms on top of the soil.
4. Wrap the bottom one third of the container in black paper.
5. Put the container in a warm, sunny place.
6. Each day for two weeks, remove the black paper to make a drawing of the container and any changes that are taking place.

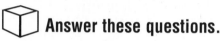 **Answer these questions.**

1. What happened to the earthworms?

_____

2. What happened to the seeds?

_____

3. What is the habitat of the earthworms? of the plants?

_____

_____

4. Predict what might have happened if there had been no soil in the container. Explain your prediction.

_____

_____

_____

5. Write a paragraph about the members of this community and their habitats.

_____

_____

_____

How Does Color Help Protect Animals?

Animals often use their color to hide from other animals. How does color help to protect animals? Try this activity to find out.

You will need

- ★ scissors
- ★ newspaper (filled mostly with black newsprint)
- ★ yellow construction paper

1. Cut an equal number of small squares from the newspaper and the construction paper.
2. Spread newspaper on the floor, and scatter all of the squares on the newspaper.
3. Cover one eye with your hand.
4. Pick up squares for ten seconds with your free hand.
5. Use the chart to record how many squares of each color you picked up.
6. Repeat steps 3–5 two more times.

Round	Yellow Squares	Newspaper Squares
1		
2		
3		
Totals		

Answer these questions.

1. Which color squares did you pick up most often?

_____

2. Which color could you see more easily? Why?

_____

3. What does this experiment tell you about the way color can help an animal survive?

_____

_____

How Animals Move

Many animals **migrate**. They move from place to place. Often, they are in search of food or mates.

 All the animals shown below migrate. Below each picture, write *flies*, *walks*, or *swims* to tell how the animal moves. On the second line, write the name of the body part that helps the animal move.

1.

_____

_____

2.

_____

_____

3.

_____

_____

4.

_____

_____

5.

_____

_____

6.

_____

_____

Animals on the Move

Answer these questions.

1. What are three reasons that animals migrate?

_____

_____

2. Give one example of each animal described. Use an encyclopedia if you need help.
   a. An animal that migrates from mountains in summer to valleys in winter.

   _____

   b. An animal that migrates from polar waters to warmer ocean waters.

   _____

   c. An insect that migrates from Canada to Mexico.

   _____

   d. A bird that migrates from South America to North America.

   _____

3. Compare and contrast the migration routes of the animals in the chart. Research the information in an encyclopedia or a science book.

Animal	Route	Reasons for Migration
Bighorn Sheep		
Monarch Butterflies		
Warblers		

Gray Squirrels

In the fall, gray squirrels prepare for winter. They eat a lot of nuts, acorns, and seeds. Their bodies become plump. Their fur thickens. These body changes will help the squirrels stay warm during the cold winter. The squirrels don't eat all their food. They bury some of it. The buried food will feed them in the winter when food is difficult to find.

When the days grow cold, the gray squirrels go into their winter homes. They will spend the winter in a hole in a tree. There, in the spring, the females give birth and raise their young. At first, the babies are helpless and do not leave the nest. After several weeks, however, the young squirrels are big enough to care for themselves. They go out and build their first home, a summer nest.

A squirrel places its summer nest high up in a tree. It wedges the nest against the tree trunk. Strong winds cannot easily blow it down. The nest is a ball of woven branches, leaves, and bark. One side of the nest has a hole for a door. The squirrel lines the inside with soft moss and grass. The finished nest makes a nearly waterproof sleeping place. Often, squirrels build several smaller homes in other trees. These homes are used as hideouts from enemies and as resting spots.

Young squirrels may spend their first winter with their parents. The next year, however, they raise their own families.

Write *true* or *false* on the line to answer each question.

_____ **1.** Gray squirrels eat nuts, acorns, and seeds.

_____ **2.** Gray squirrels sleep all winter.

_____ **3.** Young squirrels live in their parents' nest until they are big enough to take care of themselves.

_____ **4.** A large ball of leaves high up in a tree might be a squirrel's nest.

_____ **5.** Gray squirrels live in different homes during the summer and the winter.

Populations

A **population** is a number of the same type of organism living in the same place. Scientists keep track of populations. They may want to know if a population needs protection. Some populations may get too large and need to be controlled. How do scientists count populations? Try this activity to get a better idea.

You will need

★ a wire coat hanger or other stiff wire bent to form a square 12 in. (30 cm) on each side

★ a ruler   ★ dried beans   ★ rope

1. Rope off an area that is 10 feet (3 m) on each side.

2. Scatter the beans within this area.

3. Close your eyes and drop your square in the roped-off area.

4. Count the number of beans in the square. Record the number in the chart below.

5. Repeat steps 3–4 four more times in different places. Add your totals and divide by 5 for an average number.

6. Estimate the number of beans in the roped-off area.

Sample	Bean Count
1	
2	
3	
4	
5	
Total	
Average	

Answer these questions.

1. Why would you use five sample bean counts instead of only one or two?

_____

_____

2. Why might it have been more difficult to estimate the population if you had used ants instead of beans?

_____

_____

Comparing Populations

Populations differ in many ways. Choose one type of animal and compare some of its populations. For example, you may choose frogs. There are many different types of frogs, from tree frogs to poison dart frogs. They all have certain similarities, but they differ in many ways, as well. Many of their differences help them survive in their particular environment.

Answer these questions.

1. What animal did you choose? _____

2. What are some of the characteristics that all of these animals have in common?

_____

_____

_____

3. What are some of the differences between the different populations?

_____

_____

_____

4. Illustrate and color two of the animals you studied. Draw arrows to point out their differences and similarities and tell what they are.

Differences in Populations

Members of the same population can be very different from each other. Certain **traits** may vary a great deal. In this activity, you will compare some traits of each member of your family.

You will need

- ☆ a tape measure   ☆ bathroom scale

📦 **Fill in the chart below based on your measurements and observations of each member of your family. (You may include aunts, uncles, and grandparents, as well.)**

Family Member	Height	Weight	Hair Color	Eye Color	Shoe Size
Father	6' 2"	175 lbs	black	brown	12

What are some differences and similarities you found among the members of your family? Write about what you learned on another sheet of paper.

Population Explosions

Sometimes populations grow in size rapidly. The chart below shows changes in the human population.

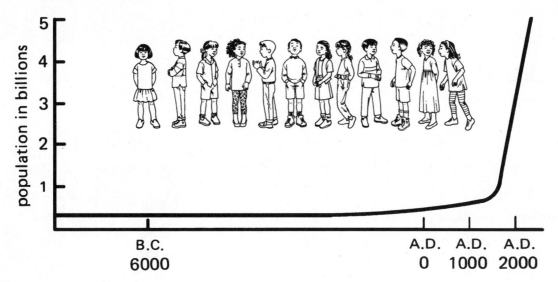

 Answer these questions.

1. What has happened to the human population in the last 1,000 years?

   _____

   _____

2. What would happen if a new student joined your class each school day for the next month?

   _____

   _____

   _____

3. There is a deer population on an island. The fox population eats deer. However, the fox population is dying from a disease. What do you think will happen to the deer population? Why?

   _____

   _____

   _____

   _____

   _____

Populations in Fossils

In this activity, you will compare two populations of fossils. A **fossil** is the remains of an organism that lived a long time ago. The fossils shown here were found in rocks.

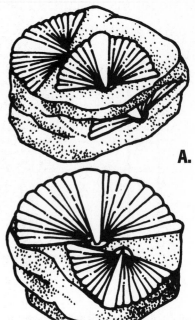

A.

B.

You will need

★ a metric ruler

1. Measure the size of each fossil in population A. Write each measurement in the chart below.

2. Measure the size of each fossil in population B. Write each measurement in the chart below.

3. Add up the measurements of population A. Divide by the number of fossils you measured. This is the average size of population A. Record this measurement.

4. Repeat step 3 for population B.

Population	A	B
size of fossil	1. 2. 3.	1. 2.

Answer these questions.

1. In which population are the fossils larger? _____

2. What might be some reasons to explain this difference?

_____

_____

Communities

Populations that live in one area and interact with each other form **communities**. If two populations interact in a way that benefits them both, it is called mutualism.

 Answer these questions.

1. What habitats are shown below?

A   **B**   **C**

_____

_____

_____

2. Describe an example of mutualism.

_____

_____

_____

_____

_____

 On another sheet of paper, draw a picture showing a community. Include at least two populations of plants and two populations of animals.

Food Makers

Communities consist of food makers, or **producers**, food takers, or consumers, and decomposers.

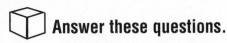 **Answer these questions.**

1. Identify the producers in the community in the picture.

   _____

   _____

   _____

2. Tell which of the following organisms are producers by writing the letter *P* next to them.

   _____ tomato   _____ weed

   _____ grass   _____ worm

   _____ squirrel   _____ potato

   _____ algae   _____ bee

3. Study this drawing of a plant. Label the places where the plant stores food.

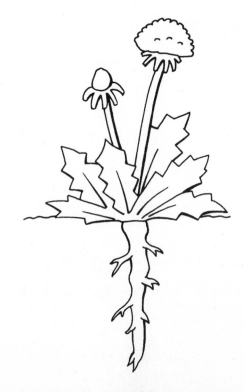

Plants Make Food

Plants store energy from the Sun, which is transferred to the organisms that eat the plants. Plants make their own food through the process of **photosynthesis**. Photosynthesis occurs when sunlight shines on the green surface of a plant. The chlorophyll inside the leaves takes in the energy from the Sun. The chlorophyll in the leaf is contained in small structures called chloroplasts. The chlorophyll uses the energy to change carbon dioxide and water into a simple sugar called glucose. Plants use this sugar as food. As a result of photosynthesis, plants give off oxygen into the air. The oxygen is a waste product of photosynthesis.

Answer the questions.

1. What is photosynthesis?

_____

_____

_____

_____

2. How are chlorophyll and chloroplasts related?

_____

_____

_____

_____

_____

GO ON TO THE NEXT PAGE ☞

Plants Make Food, p. 2

3. Label the diagram to describe the steps of photosynthesis.

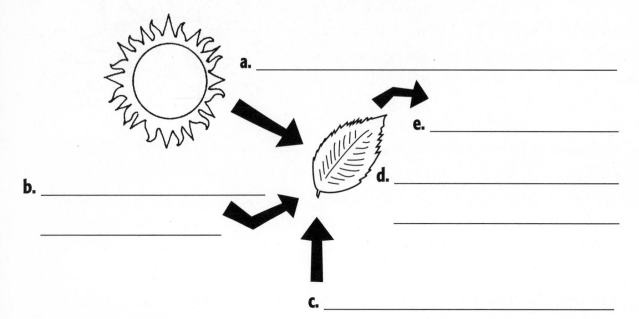

a. _____

e. _____

b. _____

_____

d. _____

_____

c. _____

Read the following paragraph. Complete the sentences. Choose words from the box, and write them on the lines.

farmers	sunlight	experiments	nutrients	water

Plants grow in different ways, depending on what kind of plants they

are, what types of 4)_____ are in the soil, the

amount of 5)_____ they get, and the amount of

6)_____ they receive. You can find out what the best

growing conditions are for plants by doing 7)_____

that test each need. Farmers have been doing experiments like that for thousands of

years. 8) _____ are the people who grow our food.

Food Takers

Food takers are also known as **consumers**. They eat the food made by the producers.

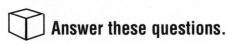 **Answer these questions.**

1. Identify at least three animals that are:

   a. herbivores (plant eaters) _____

   _____

   b. carnivores (meat eaters) _____

   _____

   c. omnivores (plant and meat eaters) _____

   _____

2. In the picture below, identify a herbivore, a carnivore, and an omnivore. Write *herbivore, carnivore,* or *omnivore* under the correct picture. Use an encyclopedia if you need help.

   _____   _____   _____

3. The chart below is a community chart. In a community chart, the plants are on the bottom, the herbivores are in the middle, and the carnivores belong at the top. Where do the following organisms belong on the chart? Write their names in the correct positions: grasshopper, chipmunk, grass, nuts, berries, robin, hawk, fox.

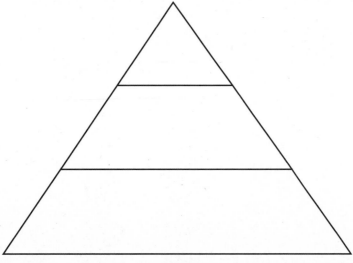

The Decomposers

The third group in a community is made of **decomposers**. When the producers and the consumers die, they begin to change; they rot and decay. The decomposers get their food from wastes and dead organisms. Molds, yeast, and bacteria break down the dead matter and give off carbon dioxide. The carbon dioxide is then used by green plants to make food.

Answer these questions.

1. What are three organisms that break down dead organisms?

_____

2. A squirrel dies in a forest. What will happen to the squirrel?

_____

_____

3. Make a diagram showing a decomposition ➞ producer ➞ consumer cycle. Use the following labels in your diagram:
   a. animals and plants die
   b. decomposers break down dead organisms
   c. materials return to soil and are used by plants to make new food
   d. animals eat plants

Observing Decomposers

Decomposers break down dead organisms. Try this activity to see what decomposers do.

You will need

☆ 2 banana slices ☆ 2 plastic sandwich bags ☆ yeast

1. Place a slice of banana into each bag.

2. Sprinkle some yeast onto one of the slices.

3. Close the bags tightly. Mark the bag with the yeast in it.

4. Watch the bags for five days. Write your observations about the differences between the two banana slices.

Day 1: _____

Day 2: _____

Day 3: _____

Day 4: _____

Day 5: _____

Write a paragraph describing what happened to the banana slices. Explain how you know that yeast is a decomposer.

_____

_____

_____

_____

_____

_____

_____

The Food Cycle

The **food cycle** includes the three groups in a community. The producers make food. The consumers eat the food. The decomposers break down dead producers and consumers. The decomposers make products that the producers use to make food. The cycle continues.

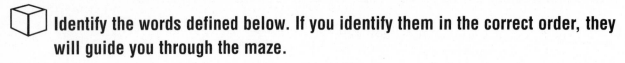 **Identify the words defined below. If you identify them in the correct order, they will guide you through the maze.**

1. Makes own food

_____

2. Tall water plants

_____

3. Floating water plant

_____

4. Foods made by green plants

_____

5. Eats plants or animals

_____

6. Eats only plants

_____

7. Eats only animals

_____

8. Eats both plants and animals

_____

9. To become rotten

_____

10. Feeds on wastes

_____

Food Chains

A **food chain** is the relationship between producers, consumers, and decomposers. It describes the order in which an organism uses a lower organism for food. For example, an insect eats a plant. A chicken eats an insect. A person eats a chicken. The food chain would be:

plant > insect > chicken > person

 Answer these questions.

1. Draw food chains for the following:

a. bird, leaf, insect _____

b. chipmunk, nuts, hawk _____

c. mouse, snake, leaf _____

2. Put each of the above food chains in the community charts drawn below. What organisms should be added to each community chart?

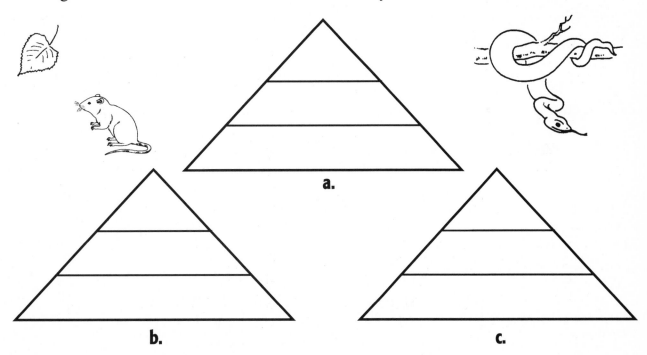

a.

b.   c.

3. A girl is eating a hamburger. Make a food chain for the meat the girl is eating. Go back as far as you can in the food chain to show the source of energy for the girl.

_____

_____

_____

Balance of Nature

Study the graph below. It shows the population of hare and lynx in Canada. The hare is the **prey** of the lynx. The lynx is a **predator**. The rise and fall in numbers of each animal tell an interesting story.

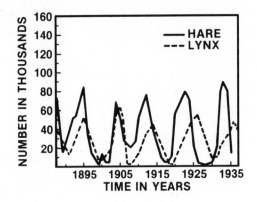

Answer these questions.

1. As the number of hares increases, what happens to the number of lynx?

_____

2. As the number of hares decreases, what happens to the number of lynx?

_____

3. Explain why the above events might be true. _____

_____

4. What do you think might happen if 10,000 lynx were brought into this area all at

once? _____

_____

_____

5. What do you think might happen if all of the lynx were killed?

_____

_____

6. Do you see that there is a balance between predators and prey? Explain.

_____

_____

Changing the Balance

Sometimes, food chains overlap. Organisms in one food chain are part of another food chain. The overlapping food chains are called **food webs**.

 **Answer these questions.**

1. Look at the food web shown below. What changes would occur if the wolves and puma were killed off?

   _____

   _____

   _____

   _____

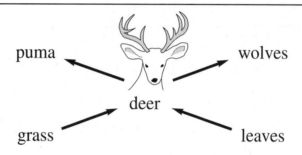

2. In the above food web, does killing off the wolves and puma help nature? Why?

   _____

   _____

3. What would happen to an insect population in a forest if all the birds died?

   _____

   What would happen to the plants in the forest community?

   _____

4. Are predators helpful in a community? How?

   _____

   _____

   _____

   _____

How Nature Helps Balance Populations

Often, nature works to keep populations in balance. Without balance, some part of the population could grow out of control. Such growth would cause problems for other parts of the population.

 Study the chart. Use the information in the chart to answer the questions. Then, make a bar graph using the data in the chart.

A RABBIT POPULATION	
Year	Population Size (in thousands)
1920	20
1921	60
1922	65
1923	75
1924	60
1925	20

1. During which year were the most plants probably eaten by the rabbits?

_____

2. What do you think probably happened to the plants during that year?

_____

_____

3. How would the smaller number of plants affect the rabbit population?

_____

_____

4. How did nature help balance the rabbit population?

_____

_____

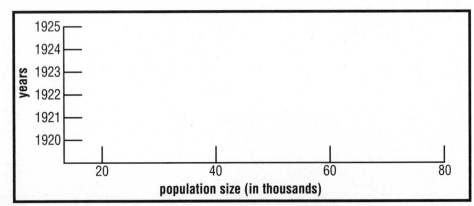

What Type of Consumer Are You?

You are a consumer. You probably eat many kinds of foods.

Make a list of everything you ate yesterday. If a food had more than one ingredient, try to list each ingredient separately. Enter the foods in the chart. Check off whether each food came from a plant or an animal.

Food	Ingredients	Plant	Animal

Answer these questions.

1. Did most of the things you ate come from animals or did they come from plants?

_____

_____

2. Would your answer be the same for the foods you have eaten so far today?

_____

_____

3. Are you a herbivore, a carnivore, or an omnivore? Explain your answer.

_____

_____

_____

People Affect Communities

The things that people do can affect communities. The effects can be good or bad.

 **Answer these questions.**

1. Make a food web for the following organisms: grass, corn, wheat, radishes, beans, chickens, cattle, rabbits, foxes, humans, hawks, decomposers. Draw the food web in the community chart.

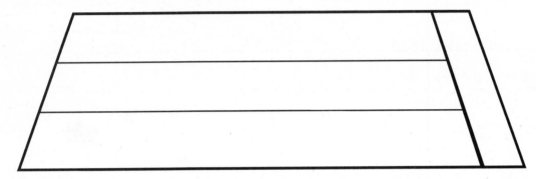

2. An ecologist was asked to make a report about the community shown below. What problems do you think the ecologist would identify for this community?

_____

_____

3. What food chains would be affected in the above community?

_____

_____

_____

How Do Oil Spills Affect the Environment?

Oil spills usually have a harmful effect on the environment. Try this activity to see how.

┌─ **You will need** ──────────────
│ ☆ newspaper   ☆ a bird feather
│ ☆ motor oil   ☆ water
│ ☆ mineral oil   ☆ a brush
└──────────────────────────────────

1. Spread the newspaper on your desk.

2. Examine the bird feather. Note its appearance and weight.

3. Coat the feather with motor oil. Observe the effect of the motor oil on the feather.

4. Now, using water, mineral oil, and a brush, try to clean the motor oil off the feather.

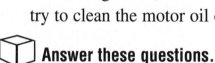 **Answer these questions.**

1. Describe the feather before it was coated with oil.

_____

2. Describe the feather after it was coated with oil.

_____

3. What effect did your cleaning have on the feather?

_____

4. Write a paragraph describing other effects of oil spills that may be harmful.

_____

_____

_____

_____

_____

_____

_____

_____

Pollution Control

Burning is a chemical reaction. When a piece of wood is burned, carbon dioxide, other gases, tar, and carbon are released into the air. These substances can cause the air to be polluted. Cars burn gasoline in their engines. The exhaust contains products that can also cause **pollution**. In the 1970s, state and federal laws were passed requiring cars to have pollution-control devices placed on the engines. Try this activity to learn more about pollution.

You will need

☆ a candle
☆ metal jar lid
☆ 4 x 4 cm piece of metal screen
☆ a spring-type clothespin

1. Place a candle on the metal jar lid.

2. With the help of an adult, light the candle.

3. Notice the orange flame and the smoke. The candle is releasing products into the air. Most of these products cannot be seen.

4. Hold the corner of the piece of metal screen in place with a spring-type clothespin.

5. Lower the screen onto the candle flame.

Answer these questions.

1. What did you see happen? _____

_____

2. What is on the screen that was not there before? _____

_____

3. This same product is released by a car engine. What would happen if all cars

released this material into the air? _____

_____

_____

Where Can You Find Air Pollution?

Are some places more likely to have **air pollution**? Do this activity to find out.

You will need

- ☆ three plastic squares (about 1 in. x 2 in. or 3 cm x 6 cm)
- ☆ a crayon
- ☆ a sheet of white paper
- ☆ petroleum jelly
- ☆ a magnifying glass

1. With the crayon, label the squares **A**, **B**, and **C**.

2. Use your finger to coat each square with a thin layer of petroleum jelly.

3. Put square A in a drawer. Put square B on a windowsill in your classroom. Put square C on a windowsill outdoors.

4. Leave the squares for 24 hours. Then, collect them. Put them on the white paper. Examine them with the magnifying glass.

Answer these questions.

1. Which square showed the most dust and dirt?

_____

2. Which square showed the least dust and dirt?

_____

3. Are dust and dirt in the air? Explain.

_____

_____

_____

4. What could be the sources of the dust and the dirt on each plastic square?

_____

_____

_____

Pollution Puzzle

Air pollution is harmful to plants, animals, and people.
Air pollution can cause people to become sick.

 Use the following words to complete the puzzle.

carbon dioxide	coal	filters	lungs	exhaust
air pollution	gases	death	eyes	sunlight

ACROSS

1. Too much ____ in the air causes air pollution.
5. Factories burn ____, which causes pollution.
7. Air pollution makes the ____ sting.
9. If the air is polluted, less ____ reaches a plant's leaves.
10. Cars pollute the air by putting many ____ in the air.

DOWN

2. When there is no clean air, we say there is ____.
3. Car ____ systems can cause pollution.
4. Special ____ are needed in exhaust systems to cut down on pollution.
6. Air pollution can even cause ____ if people are exposed for long periods of time.
8. When we breathe, whatever is in the air enters our ____.

Beaches: Clean or Dirty?

What happens to the waste your community produces? Unfortunately, some of it may go into the ocean. Because the ocean is so large, people used to think that nothing could harm it. A little trash seemed simply to disappear in the giant body of water. In the past, the United States dumped millions of tons of wastes into the ocean each year. These wastes included chemicals as well as plant and animal matter. In addition, sewage was allowed to wash into the ocean.

Now, only properly "treated" wastes are allowed to flow to the ocean. For example, sewage plants are allowed to put treated water into rivers and streams that eventually drain into the ocean. But there are still problems. One problem is the uncertainty of how much waste is too much. Another problem is that wastes are often not treated completely. When there is too much rain in an area, sewage can pour out of a treatment plant before it has had time to be processed completely. This undertreated sewage may then flow into the ocean.

In the past, few people were aware of the problems of "ocean dumping." But wastes are now washing up on the nation's shorelines. Pollution in the form of harmful bacteria has made some beaches unsafe for swimming.

Some of the wastes that have washed onto the shore come from illegal ocean dumping. In the past, most garbage was simply hauled to a local dump. But now trash and garbage are taken to landfills that charge a fee. Landfills will not accept some dangerous materials. To avoid the cost and the rules of landfills, some haulers dump trash and garbage into the ocean. Some of the wastes that are illegally dumped in this way are the most dangerous. Included in this group are medical wastes that are very expensive to handle safely. Large amounts of dangerous medical wastes, including hypodermic needles that have been used to give "shots," are dumped into the ocean. As a result, needles wash up on shore. These needles are very dangerous. A person who is stuck with one of the needles can become very sick.

Other types of solid waste also wash up on shore. Some of these are ordinary things, such as plastic bags or the rings that hold a six-pack of soft-drink cans. These bits of trash can be deadly for ocean and shore animals.

GO ON TO THE NEXT PAGE ☞

Beaches: Clean or Dirty?, p. 2

Animals such as dolphins often mistake empty plastic bags for jellyfish, one of their foods. Many dolphins choke to death each year from swallowing plastic bags. Plastic rings are also killers. The rings can get tangled around the necks of diving birds. Then, the birds can't swallow food, and they strangle or starve.

Because the problems of ocean dumping and water pollution have become so bad, people are trying to make a change. Dumping trash into the ocean is now against the law, and people who are caught doing so are punished. Many people work to clean up beaches. Often school and community groups and Scouts volunteer to clean up beaches. In areas where medical wastes are not a problem, people pick up ordinary trash and have it hauled away. You might see if there's a group that cleans up shores or beaches in your area. If not, think about starting a group cleanup project. You can also help by taking gloves and a garbage bag along the next time you go to the beach with friends or your family. You should put on your gloves before you begin to collect trash. Put the trash in your garbage bag. Every little bit that you can do will help.

Answer these questions.

1. How do beaches get polluted?

_____

_____

2. What are some dangerous types of wastes that might be found on a beach?

_____

_____

3. What types of waste in the ocean and on the shore are dangerous to animals?

Explain. _____

_____

_____

A Balanced Diet

Scientists have studied the amounts of foods that are necessary for people to eat in order to get enough nutrients, vitamins, and minerals. The food pyramid below shows how much of each type of food people should eat each day to stay healthy.

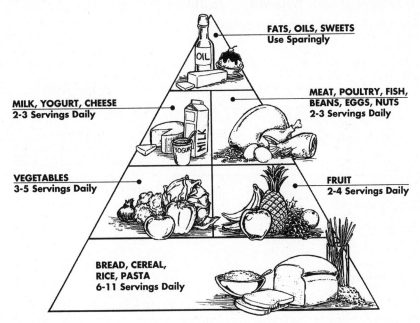

Using the information provided in the food pyramid, make a menu for one day. Be sure that your menu includes the number of servings that are recommended in the pyramid.

BREAKFAST		LUNCH		DINNER		SNACKS	
Food	Type	Food	Type	Food	Type	Food	Type

Total your servings for each group. Does your menu follow the pyramid recommendations?

Bread/Cereal Group: _____   Vegetable Group: _____

Fruit Group: _____   Milk Group: _____

Meat Group: _____   Fats Group: _____

How Is Your Diet?

Do you eat a **balanced diet**? Try this activity to find out about your eating habits.

 Keep track of what you eat for three days. Then, compare your diet with the diet that is recommended on the food pyramid.

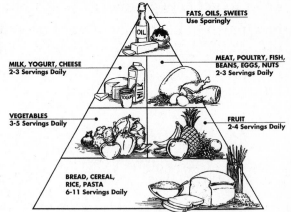

Day 1	Breakfast	Lunch	Dinner	Snacks
Day 2	Breakfast	Lunch	Dinner	Snacks
Day 3	Breakfast	Lunch	Dinner	Snacks

 Answer these questions.

1. Which food do you need to eat more of? _____

2. Which food do you need to eat less of? _____

3. Do you have a healthy diet? _____

Reading Food Package Labels

It is important to know what is in the foods we buy. Learn what food package labels can tell you.

┌─ **You will need** ────────────────────────────────┐
☆ 3 cereal boxes (of different kinds of cereals)
└──┘

1. Find the Nutrition Information per Serving Chart on each box.

2. Write the name of each cereal and the serving size.

   a. Name _____

      Serving Size _____

   b. Name _____

      Serving Size _____

   c. Name _____

      Serving Size _____

Answer these questions on another sheet of paper.

1. Which cereal has the most calories in one serving?

2. Which cereal has the most protein in one serving?

3. Which cereal has the most carbohydrates in one serving?

4. Which cereal has the most fat in one serving?

5. Which nutrients are listed on each box?

6. Are there any vitamins listed that provide less than five percent of the RDA (Recommended Daily Allowance)? If so, which ones are they?

7. Find the list of ingredients. Does any cereal list sugar as one of the first three ingredients? What does that tell you?

8. Which of these cereals has the most fiber in one serving?

9. Do you think any of these cereals are empty-calorie foods? Why or why not?

10. Which of these cereals is best for you? Why?

To Be a Vegetarian

You've probably heard about vegetarians, but you may not know exactly what being a vegetarian means. Someone who is a vegetarian follows a vegetarian diet and eats no meat of any kind. That means eating no flesh of any animal, including chicken and fish.

People usually follow a vegetarian diet for one of two reasons: either for moral reasons or for health concerns. Many people feel that it's not right to eat other animals. They may also feel that eating meat is a wasteful practice when so many people in the world do not have enough to eat. This reasoning is based on the fact that cattle are fed grain that could be used to feed people. As you might know from reading about food webs, energy is lost as it goes from one living thing to the next. In other words, a cow takes in much more energy than a human or another animal could gain from eating its flesh.

Many people follow a vegetarian diet because of health concerns. A vegetarian diet is one way of lowering the amount of fat a person eats. The traditional American meat-centered diet is very high in fat. And high-fat diets have been shown to be a factor in many diseases, including heart disease and cancer.

Some vegetarians avoid not only meat but also animal products, such as eggs and milk. This diet is harder to follow because many foods, from breads to salads, may contain ingredients made from milk or eggs. Other vegetarians believe it is okay to eat animal products as long as the animal is not harmed. These people get protein from foods such as yogurt, cottage cheese, and other milk products. Some vegetarians also eat products that contain eggs.

Vegetarians who eat egg and milk products can easily get enough protein, an important part of a healthful diet. Those who do not eat any eggs or milk must be more careful to make sure they get enough protein in their diets. Many foods, such as beans, nuts, and grains, have high levels of protein. But a variety of these foods must be eaten together to provide the proteins the body needs to stay healthy. Eating beans and rice together provides this kind of protein.

GO ON TO THE NEXT PAGE ☞

To Be a Vegetarian, p. 2

In the past, it was thought that people needed to eat large amounts of protein. Now, research has shown that people need less protein and more grains, fruits, and vegetables. The new food pyramid shows the suggested amount of different foods. The large base of the pyramid shows those foods needed in the greatest amounts. As you go up the pyramid, you find foods that you need in smaller and smaller amounts.

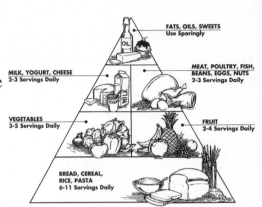

Answer these questions.

1. What is a vegetarian?

_____

_____

2. Why might it be more healthful to be a vegetarian than to eat a traditional American diet?

_____

_____

3. According to the food pyramid, how many servings of bread or cereal should you eat each day? how many servings of vegetables? of fruits?

_____

_____

4. Suggest a menu for a vegetarian meal. If you like, it may contain milk and egg products.

_____

_____

Teeth, Muscles, and Bones

Eating the right foods is only part of what you can do to take care of yourself. You must be sure to brush and floss your teeth and see a dentist for regular checkups. You need to exercise to maintain healthy muscles and bones.

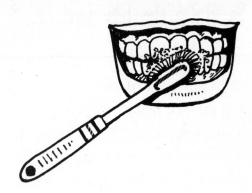

🔲 **Take this test to see if you know how to keep your teeth, muscles, and bones healthy. Write *T* if the statement is true or *F* if it is false.**

_____ **1.** If you brush your teeth enough, you do not need to floss.

_____ **2.** You only need to brush your teeth if you eat candy.

_____ **3.** You should brush your teeth every time you eat.

_____ **4.** Your muscles will become weak if you do not use them.

_____ **5.** Muscles will become bigger and stronger with use.

_____ **6.** Exercise has nothing to do with posture.

_____ **7.** Exercise can help your bones.

_____ **8.** Exercise will help you sleep at night.

_____ **9.** Exercise helps your lungs and heart to stay strong.

_____ **10.** Exercise is not important for your bones.

🔲 **Answer these questions on another sheet of paper.**

11. Name three things that you can do to keep your teeth healthy.

12. Name three things that you can do to keep your muscles healthy.

13. How can healthy, strong muscles help your bones?

Why Warm Up and Cool Down?

Have you ever been to a football game? Do you remember seeing the players warm up? Cold, tight muscles should be warmed up and stretched little by little. This prevents muscle injuries and muscle soreness. There are two types of warm-ups. General warm-ups are for the whole body. These exercises should take between three to five minutes. They should include some stretching, some calisthenics (like jumping jacks), and some walking and jogging. There are also specific warm-ups. These exercises help the body get ready for the sport. For example, in softball, players may throw the ball back and forth.

Cool-down exercises are just as important as warm-ups. Cool-down exercises take about ten minutes. You should gradually slow down your activity. For example, cool down after jogging by walking. Stretching should also be part of the cool-down exercises. This can prevent muscle soreness.

In the first column, make a list of sports or athletics that you engage in. In the other columns, make a list of warm-up and cool-down exercises you can do.

Sports	Warm Up	Cool Down

Healthful Hiking

How would you like to go for a hike in the woods? Exploring outside can be even more interesting than learning about nature from books. You can hear the calls of the birds and see the shapes of their nests. You can see the colors of leaves and the way they fall silently in autumn. In exploring the woods, you will also get fresh air and exercise. Hiking in the outdoors can improve both your mind and your body.

Although there's much to be gained by going outdoors, there are also risks. The best way to be safe is to plan ahead. You need to think about what you will probably find on your outing and about what might go wrong. For example, if you go hiking in the summer, you will probably get hot and thirsty. But you may also need to take precautions to avoid contact with poison ivy or other poisonous plants.

There are a few things to do before you go on any hike. The most important is to let others know where you'll be going. That way, if you should run into trouble, others will know where to look for you. Second, follow a trail. Even though you may think you'll be able to find your way back, the safest path is the one that's marked. Away from the path, you could wander for hours before finding your way back. If possible, take along a trail map. Third, always wear the right kind of shoes for the area of your hike. Most often, the best shoes are sturdy hiking boots with nonslip soles. Regular shoes do not support your feet, and they make it difficult to climb up rocky areas. Fourth, take along a container of water.

The next part of your planning should be thinking about the season and the possible changes in weather. For example, in the winter a sudden change in the weather might bring a cold rain or a snowstorm. Wearing many layers of warm clothes and packing a waterproof poncho can help you stay warm and dry. Your body also needs extra energy when you get cold. Taking along snacks, such as nuts and raisins, can give you the energy you need. In addition, the Sun sets early in the winter. Planning a hike that is short enough to be over before nightfall is very important.

GO ON TO THE NEXT PAGE ☞

Healthful Hiking, p. 2

For a summer hike, you will need to wear sturdy hiking boots and layers of lightweight clothing. You can remove layers as the day warms up. In some places, you may want to wear long pants and shirts with long sleeves as protection from certain plants and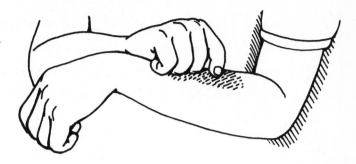
insects. In some areas of the country, ticks and insects carry diseases. Proper clothing and insect repellent can help protect you from these pests. After your hike, you should check your body for ticks. If you find them, ask an adult or your doctor about removing them. Clothing can also help protect you from poisonous plants, such as poison ivy, poison oak, and poison sumac. If you think you may have come in contact with any of these poisonous plants, wash your skin with special soap available at a drugstore. Washing with regular soap will not remove the plant's oils from your skin.

Answer these questions.

1. What four things should you do to prepare for any hike?

_____

_____

2. What are some risks in winter hiking? How should you prepare for each?

_____

_____

3. What are some problems that you need to consider when you plan a summer hike?

_____

_____

4. How would you plan a hike for this weekend? What would you need to wear? What would you take along?

_____

_____

What Keeps You Healthy?

A habit is an activity you do so many times that it becomes automatic. Brushing your teeth every day is a good habit. Smoking cigarettes is a bad habit. All of your habits together are called your lifestyle. Some lifestyle habits can help you stay healthy. You need to begin good health habits when you are young. This will help you stay healthy for a long time.

Many scientists have studied lifestyles. They have discovered that seven health habits are very important. Following the habits listed below can help you stay healthy. Do you follow all these habits?

1. Never smoke cigarettes.

2. Exercise every day.

3. Use little or no alcohol.

4. Sleep seven or eight hours every night.

5. Eat breakfast every day.

6. Do not eat many snacks between meals.

7. Keep your weight right—not too thin and not too fat.

Below are scrambled words about health habits. Decode the words and write them in the spaces to the right. Then, use the circled letters to find the secret word.

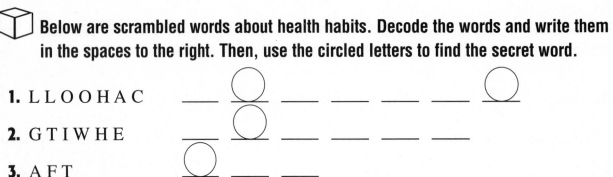

1. L L O O H A C

2. G T I W H E

3. A F T

4. R A K E B A F S T

5. Y L E T H A H

6. P S E E L

7. X I E E E C S R

Now, unscramble the circled letters to form the secret word.

____ ____ ____ ____ ____ ____ ____

What's Your First Aid IQ?

First aid is the immediate care that is given to an injured person. Sometimes, if the injury is a small one, the right first aid may be the only care that is needed. Would you know what to do for a burn, a bruise, a small cut, or a deep wound?

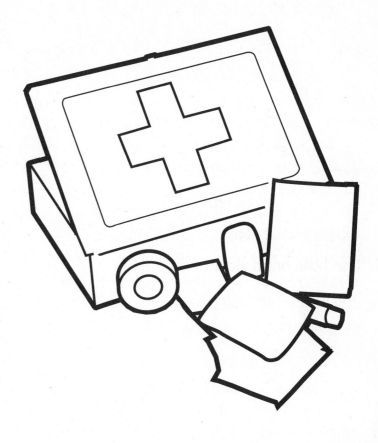

Burns damage or destroy some skin cells. If the burn is small and does not have blisters, you can run cold water over it. You might also hold ice against the burned area. If the burn has blisters or is large, a doctor should be called. Even a small burn is bad if it has blisters.

Ice or cold cloths are good first aid for bruises. The cold helps reduce swelling and cuts down on the pain.

First aid for cuts is very important. A small cut should be washed with soap and water. You should always put a clean bandage over the cut to keep harmful germs out. If the cut is deep, you may have lots of bleeding. You will have to hold a clean pad tightly over the wound to stop the bleeding until you can get to a doctor.

Always try to keep the injured person calm. A person can make the injury worse by becoming upset. Tell the injured person that everything will be all right. Take care of the wound if you can. Otherwise, stay with the injured person until an adult or medical help arrives.

GO ON TO THE NEXT PAGE ☞

What's Your First Aid IQ?, p. 2

Complete the crossword puzzle about first aid.

ACROSS

2. ____ ____ is the immediate care given to an injured person.
5. For a small burn with no blisters, run cold ____ on it at once.
6. Put ice or cold cloths on a ____ to cut down on the swelling.
9. A clean pad should be held ____ over a deep wound until you get to a doctor.
10. Ice on a burn or bruise will help cut down on ____.
11. If a burn is blistered or deep, the person should be cared for by a ____.

DOWN

1. Always put a clean ____ over a cut.
3. Sometimes, if the ____ is a small one, first aid is all that is needed.
4. You should put ____ or cold water on a burn.
6. If a small burn has a ____, it is a bad burn.
7. A small cut should be washed with ____ and water.
8. ____ damage or destroy some skin cells.

Plants: Harmful and Helpful

You may have learned the hard way about some harmful plants. If you've ever come back from an outing in the woods with an itchy rash, you may have learned firsthand about poison ivy, poison oak, or poison sumac. These plants have oils in their leaves that cause an allergic reaction in most people. If you brush against the leaves, your body reacts to the oil. First, you get a rash; then it starts to itch. It usually takes about a week for the rash to go away. The oils in these plants are so strong that you can get a rash from them if they're burning and smoke touches you!

Most poisonous plants are not harmful unless they are eaten. What may surprise you is that people eat poisonous plants by accident all the time. Think about small children. They will put almost anything in their mouths, and they often eat house plants. Chewing a single leaf of the popular house plant called Diffenbachia, or dumb cane, can cause a child to be unable to speak for a while. If larger amounts are eaten, the leaves can cause internal bleeding and damage to the liver and kidneys.

There are many other common poisonous plants. For example, hemlock, a flowering shrub with white flowers, was used as a poison by the ancient Greeks. This plant is not native to North America, but it was brought here and does grow in the wild. If this plant is eaten, even in small amounts, it can paralyze or kill a person or an animal.

Many plants affect the heart. They either speed up the heartbeat or slow it down. Often these effects are helpful. However, if the plant is eaten, the effects can kill a person. For example, oleander is a plant that has beautiful flowers and is often used on roadsides and in yards. There is a substance in the leaves of this plant that can damage the heart. Foxglove is a beautiful flower that is often found in gardens. It contains a substance that is very helpful in treating heart conditions. However, if a person or an animal eats the plant, it can be deadly.

GO ON TO THE NEXT PAGE 👉

Name _____   Date _____

Plants: Harmful and Helpful, p. 2

These plants are just a few of the many plants that can be helpful or harmful. As you know, any medicine can be harmful if you take too much. And when you eat a plant that contains a medicine, you almost always get too much.

There is an evergreen tree that grows in Washington and Oregon called the Pacific yew. It is so poisonous that eating any of its leaves or seeds can cause the heart to stop. There are no symptoms for a doctor to treat; the person or animal that eats it dies quickly. But the bark of this tree has been found to contain a substance that can be used to treat some kinds of cancer. In fact, it is better treatment for these cancers than anything else that we know about!

Answer these questions.

1. How can poison ivy affect people?

_____

_____

2. What are three poisonous plants? How do they affect you? Give examples.

_____

_____

_____

3. What do the Pacific yew tree and foxglove have in common?

_____

_____

4. Why might it be a good idea to learn about the different kinds of plants that can be found in the woods before you go on a hike?

_____

_____

Science Grade 4

Answer Key

Pages 4–6
1. T, **2.** F, **3.** T, **4.** T, **5.** T, **6.** F,
7. B, **8.** A, **9.** B, **10.** C, **11.** B,
12. D, **13.** T, **14.** F, **15.** T, **16.** F,
17. T, **18.** F, **19.** A, **20.** B, **21.** A,
22. A, **23.** D, **24.** A, **25.** F, **26.** T,
27. F, **28.** F, **29.** F, **30.** T, **31.** B,
32. C, **33.** D, **34.** A, **35.** B, **36.** C

Pages 13–14
1. F, **2.** T, **3.** F, **4.** F, **5.** F, **6.** T,
7. T, **8.** T, **9.** D, **10.** B, **11.** A,
12. A, **13.** D, **14.** C, **15.** B, **16.** C,
17. D, **18.** D, **19.** A, **20.** B

Pages 15–16
1. The total force is 100 newtons + 75 newtons = 175 newtons. The wagon will move forward., **2.** The wagon will move backward because Erin is applying a greater force than Mikal is., **3.** The rope will move toward Kate's team., **4.** 260 newtons – 60 newtons = 200 newtons; The rope will move toward Justin's side because his team is pulling with greater force., **5.** The boxcar will not move because the two forces are equal, or balanced., **6.** The total force on the boxcar is 2,000 newtons. The boxcar will move to the right.

Page 17
Answers will vary.

Page 18
1. nutcracker; cracks open nuts, **2.** can opener; opens lids on cans, **3.** shovel; helps to dig dirt, **4.** hammer; pounds in and pulls out nails, **5.** pruning shears; cuts through tree branches, **6.** screwdriver; turns screws and pries open lids

Page 20
6. knitting needle: fulcrum; tube: lever, **7.** The right pan sinks and the left pan rises. The force of the quarter is pushing it down., **8.** The left pan sinks slightly and the right pan rises. The downward force of the penny. The quarter; The pan with the quarter in it is still lower than the one with the penny., **9.** Answers will vary.

Page 21
1. The angle made using 3 books., **2.** The angle made using 1 book., **3.** The steeper the angle of an inclined plane, the greater the force needed to move an object up the incline.

Page 22
1. ax; separates wood, **2.** nail; separates wood, **3.** plow; separates soil

Page 23
1. inclined plane, **2.** The screw with the most threads will be easier to turn into the wood because the angle of each inclined plane is less than in the other two screws., **3.** the screw with the most threads

Page 24
1. The picture with the two pulleys makes work easier. It uses both a fixed pulley and a movable pulley. The direction of force is changed and less force is needed to raise an object., **2.** Possible answers: flagpoles, sailboats, cranes

Page 25
1. handle of screwdriver, **2.** metal stem of screwdriver, **3.** The screwdriver with the thinner handle is harder to turn; although fewer turns are used to complete the job. The wheel is smaller, so more force is needed to turn the screw in. With the thicker handle, more turns are needed to embed the screw, but it is not as hard to turn. So, the thicker handle sacrifices the distance the hand turns, but less force is required to complete the job.

Page 26
1. Both use a wheel and axle, but in the gear system, the wheel has teeth and there are generally two or more gears together., **2.** The blade turns faster than the large gear., **3.** Check students' work.

Page 27
Order: 2, 4, 3, 1; **1.** 2, **2.** 1, **3.** Only a small part touches the ground at one time., **4.** The surface of the floor is smoother.

Page 28
1. vegetable oil, **2.** There was less heat with the lubricant, and the hands felt slippery., **3.** The marbles produced less heat and were more slippery., **4.** A lubricant reduces friction by creating a slippery material between two materials.

Page 30
1. sandpaper; The surface is bumpy and rough., **2.** wax paper; The surface is smooth and flat., **3.** The rubber pads of the brakes rub on the rim of the tire, causing friction. The bike slows and stops., **4.** Rubbing causes friction and friction causes heat.

Page 31
1. The pencils and marbles act like wheels., **2.** The box without pencils or marbles caused the most friction because the total surface bottom of the box rubbed against the table., **3.** The marbles caused the least friction because their surface touched the box and table the least., **4.** Answers will vary.

Page 32
1. C, **2.** D, **3.** D, **4.** The stereo is producing sounds, which travel through the air as vibrations. When the sounds reach the glasses, the glasses vibrate as well.

Page 33
1. When the pot is struck, the sound waves hit the plastic wrap, causing it to vibrate. The rice then begins to vibrate., **2.** The rice moved slightly or not at all., **3.** The rice moved a lot., **4.** Answers will vary., **5.** When a sound is made, it moves away in a wave. As the sound wave hits other objects, it causes them to vibrate. The louder the sound, the more an object vibrates.

Page 34
1. The wax paper vibrated., **2.** Yes; The stream of air caused the wax paper to vibrate against the comb. This vibration makes a sound we can hear., **3.** Yes; The vibration of the wax paper causes it to vibrate against the lips.

Page 35
1. Solid: You could feel and hear the sound vibrations of the tuning fork more clearly as they traveled through the table., **2.** Gas; While you could faintly hear the vibrations as they moved through the air, you could not feel them.

Page 36
1. the metal pot, **2.** Yes; Sound travels better through a hard solid. Metal is a harder solid than wood., **3.** hard objects

Page 37
1. no, **2.** air, **3.** water, **4.** granite, **5.** 4,999 – 4,877 = 122 meters per second faster, **6.** 6,096 – 332 = 5,764 meters per second faster

Page 38
The answers are in the following order: 2, 5, 1, 4, 6, 3.

Page 39
1. B, **2.** C, **3.** A, **4.** D

Page 40
The answers are in the following order: 4, 1, 5, 2, 3.

Page 41
Step 3: When you hit the pan, it causes vibrations. These vibrations are sound waves that travel through the air. The sound waves make the plastic vibrate. The sugar then vibrates from the movement of the plastic., **1.** The stretched plastic is like the surface of the eardrum. It vibrates like the eardrum., **2.** Sound waves are vibrations traveling through the air. They cause the eardrum to vibrate, which sends signals to the brain. The brain reads the signals as sounds., **3.** Neither the metal pan nor the spoon were touching the plastic, so sound waves must have traveled to the plastic. As they hit the plastic, the sound waves caused the plastic to vibrate., **4.** If the sound was loud, the sugar would jump more. If it was soft, the sugar would jump very little.

Page 42
1. jackhammer, gunshots at firing range, explosion, **2.** breathing, **3.** (talking) 25 decibels – (whispering) 10 decibels = 15 decibels, **4.** Answers will vary: about 60 decibels, **5.** noisy home: 55 decibels; loud conversation: 50 decibels; movie theater: 45 decibels, **6.** Check students' graphs.

Page 43
1. An instrument called an echo sounder sends off sound waves through the water. The waves hit the bottom of the ocean and bounce back to the ship. The time it takes the sound waves to return is calculated to find how deep the ocean bottom is., **2.** 34 km, **3.** about 500 meters below the surface, **4.** about 2,000 meters, **5.** about 1,500 meters high, **6.** Possible answer: to find ancient shipwrecks.

Page 44
1. light source, **2.** reflects light, **3.** light source, **4.** light source, **5.** light source, **6.** reflects light

Page 45
1. Students should say "no," unless there is a lot of dust in the air., **2.** The water made the light beam visible., **3.** The light reflects, or bounces off, the water so the eyes can see it.

Page 46

1. Yes, **2.** The light was blocked, **3.** Possible answers: There were shadows around the circle of light on the moved card. The first card blocked all the light except where the hole was., **4.** Yes; The light was blocked when the middle card was moved. Shadows were formed around the circle of light., **5.** It is reflected or absorbed.

Page 47

1. glass 1, **2.** glasses 2 and 4, **3.** glass 3

Page 48

1. Students will see a series of images., **2.** Answers will vary, depending on the angle., **3.** The number of images decreases as the angle gets larger.

Page 49

Smooth surface: Reflection lines should be at the same angle as the incoming light.,
Uneven surface: Reflection lines will be different, depending on the surface each arrow hits.

Page 50

1. The light became brighter., **2.** The light became brighter., **3.** The mirrors can be angled so that their reflection hits one spot., **4.** Several flat mirrors can be angled so they act like one curved mirror.

Pages 51–52

1. A concave mirror curves in and a convex mirror curves out., **2.** The concave mirror is behind the lightbulb. The lightbulb reflects back to the mirror, and the beams bounce out and hit a focus spot which is brighter., **3.** The mirror is used for security. Because it gathers a wider range of beams, it can see a wider angle.,

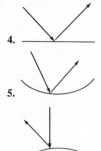

4.
5.
6.
7. flat: periscope; concave: flashlight; convex: store mirror, **8.** 5 and 6, **9.** 5

Page 53

1. The light moves in a straight path., **2.** The light beam bends., **3.** You can increase the angle of the light.

Page 54

1. Both focus light to a point., **2.** Lenses are transparent so you can see through them., **3.** Light enters one side of the lens and bends as it moves from air to glass. As the beam exits the glass, it bends a second time as it hits the air., **4.** Possible answers: telescope, microscope, eyeglasses, magnifying glass

Page 56

1. Light beams reflect from an object to a person's eye. The light passes through the cornea and the lens. These parts bend the light beams together, focusing them on the retina. The image of the object forms on the retina., **2.** Light is focused in front of the retina in nearsighted people. Light is focused behind the retina in farsighted people., **3.** The shape changes where the light is focused.

Page 57

1. The light bends as it enters the prism, separating the colors in light. The colors are bent again as they exit the prism, spreading out more., **2.** A spectrum is seven colors that make up light., **3.** Water, like glass, can bend light. A raindrop bends rays of sunlight and produces a spectrum of colors., **4.** Sunlight hits a raindrop and bends several times, making the spectrum of colors in the rainbow.

Page 58

1. White light is clear light made up of seven colors., **2.** The color reflected was the color of the paper being tested., **3.** The other colors were absorbed by the paper., **4.** The color of the object is reflected to our eyes so we can see it. The other colors are absorbed.

Page 59

1. They blend together., **2.** white

Page 60

1. A laser beam is concentrated along its length. A flashlight beam spreads out., **2.** The laser would be more accurate than entering in the prices, and it would speed up the checkout process.

Page 61

1. The candle looks like it is burning in the glass., **2.** The glass reflects the light., **3.** The glass has a smooth surface., **4.** You see the plastic glass and water., **5.** The glass is translucent.

Pages 69–70

1. F, **2.** F, **3.** T, **4.** T, **5.** F, **6.** F, **7.** e, **8.** k, **9.** h, **10.** c, **11.** a, **12.** b, **13.** j, **14.** f, **15.** d, **16.** l, **17.** i, **18.** g, **19.** A, **20.** B, **21.** C, **22.** B, **23.** B, **24.** D, **25.** B, **26.** C, **27.** A, **28.** B

Page 71

1. crust, **2.** mantle, **3.** core, Comparison: Answers will vary. Students should equate skin of apple with the crust, fleshy part with mantle, core with core.

Page 72

1. sedimentary, **2.** igneous, **3.** sedimentary, **4.** igneous, **5.** sandstone, **6.** bituminous coal

Page 73

1. sediments, **2.** 5 minutes; the height of the clay layer, **3.** 2 cm; 1.5 cm; 1 cm; 0.5 cm, **4.** No more than and probably less than 0.5 cm higher; over time, the clay settled less and less., **5.** The sediments settle out of the ocean water like the clay settled out of the water in the jar. The sediments form a layer on the ocean floor like the clay did at the bottom of the jar. Over time, the sediments continue to settle, but more slowly. In order for sedimentary rocks to form, heat and pressure must be applied, but this model shows the beginning of the process., **6.** Answers will vary. Possible response: The amount of time between observations should be based on the data being collected. Sometimes you start out with a time span and you have to change it to fit the data.

Page 74

1. igneous, sedimentary, metamorphic, **2.** igneous, **3.** sedimentary, **4.** igneous, sedimentary, metamorphic, **5.** igneous, **6.** igneous, sedimentary, **7.** igneous, **8.** sedimentary, **9.** metamorphic, **10.** sedimentary, **11.** igneous, sedimentary, metamorphic, **12.** sedimentary, **13.** sedimentary

Page 75

Step 1: The marbles should not have cracks., **1.** Each day the Sun's rays heat the exposed sides of the rocks. Each night the rocks cool off., **2.** It can crack them.

Page 76

1. Crystals form around the paper clip., **2.** As the water evaporated, the salt formed crystals on the paper clip.

Page 77

1. It prevented the addition of minerals that might be in tap water., **2.** The minerals came from the soil., **3.** Dissolve the minerals in water and add the water to a plant. Compare the growth of two plants, watering only one with minerals.

Pages 78–79

1. e, **2.** a, **3.** f, **4.** b, **5.** d, **6.** c, **7.** A, **8.** A, **9.** B, Leaf litter is present., **10.** A, There is a deep area of loamy soil.

Page 81

1. One rock wall could drop down, leaving the other rock wall higher. A normal fault could help form a mountain like this., **2.** A normal fault forms when rock walls pull away from each other. A reverse fault forms when rock walls push against each other., **3.** If this curb were on a fault line, a lateral fault could pull it apart like this.

Page 82

1. quiet, **2.** earthquakes, **3.** cracks in the ground, **4.** powerful shock wave, **5.** mud flows or rivers of mud

Page 84

Correct order: 2, 5, 4, 3, 1, 6

Page 86

1. They form from once-living things buried deep underground. They are called fossil fuels because they form from things that lived millions of years ago., **2.** It would be dangerous to people on the oil rig, and they would have to be rescued. Oil would collect in and on the water, which could cut off light and oxygen, killing many types of living things., **3.** Answers will vary but should include a discussion of potential risks versus gains.

Page 88

1. Bituminous coal would cause most of the pollution because it has a high sulfur content. This is a problem because most of the coal the U.S. produces is bituminous. This coal should not be used without pollution-control devices., **2.** It provides high heat and has a low sulfur content, so it causes less pollution., **3.** All vegetation and soil above the coal is removed, which destroys many ecosystems and the way the land looks. Some places have laws that require operators to restore the land after the coal is mined., **4.** We will have to find new ways to produce energy or to use less energy. The teacher could talk about alternate energy here, and assign students to report on different nonfossil-fuel sources of energy.

Page 89

1. by tying a string around one end of the film can and attaching a weight, **2.** Movements of both depend on movement of water or wind, **3.** wheel and axle

Page 90

Across: 1. energy, **2.** generate, **4.** water, **5.** grind, **6.** wind;
Down: 1. electric, **3.** America

Page 91

Step 4: The model would function better if it were attached or weighted at the bottom, so it wouldn't blow around in the wind.

www.svschoolsupply.com
© Steck-Vaughn Company

174

Answer Key
Science 4, SV 7936-7

Page 92
Students should correctly label layers of atmosphere. From layer nearest Earth up: troposphere, stratosphere, ionosphere, exosphere.

Page 93
1. 78%, 2. oxygen, 3. about 1%, 4. much more oxygen than carbon dioxide, 5. nitrogen

Page 94
1. They cause some nitrogen molecules to combine with oxygen molecules. Nitrates form in the soil; these get used by plants., 2. nitrogen-fixing bacteria, 3. from the soil, 4. from the plants, 5. to stay alive and to grow, 6. Bacteria help return it to the soil., 7. yes

Page 95
Students should correctly label three stages of water cycle: evaporation (near bottom), condensation (near clouds), precipitation (near rain).

Page 96
Step 6: Answers will vary but should include information about the activity setup and the water that formed on the inside of the bowl.; 1. Water beaded up (condensed) on the inside of the bowl., 2. Water inside the bowl is fresh; water in the cup is salty., 3. The warm salt water evaporated, or changed from a liquid to a gas. When the water vapor, or gas, touched the bowl, it changed back to liquid water., 4. It stayed in the cup., 5. In desalination plants, energy is needed to evaporate the water. In the activity, the energy came from the heat of the warm water., 6. Large quantities of energy are needed to produce small amounts of fresh water.

Page 97
1. higher in direct sunlight, 2. The temperature is higher over dark surfaces.

Page 98
1. The cold water flowed along the bottom, forcing the hot water up., 2. hot air mass, 3. cold air mass, 4. cold front

Page 99
1. Answers will vary., 2. Causes for altering wind direction include the nearness of other buildings and trees that deflect winds and the location of a building on a hill or in a valley.

Page 100
1. rain, 2. rain, 3. snow, 4. sleet

Page 101
1. a cloud, 2. The air is cooled by the ice cubes., 3. The water vapor in the air changes to tiny droplets of water., 4. A cloud forms when droplets of water float in the air., 5. It is cold where clouds form because clouds are made from water vapor that is cooled to become water droplets.

Page 103
1. Caribou, Chicago, and Duluth, 2. Caribou, 3. 104 cm, 4. Bakersfield and Phoenix, 5. Caribou, Chicago, and Duluth, 6. Bakersfield and Phoenix, 7. no; Dallas doesn't get enough snow.

Page 104
Students should position the symbol for low pressure slightly off the Pacific Northwest states; the symbol for snow somewhere in the area of Washington, Oregon, and Idaho; the symbol for high pressure over Texas; and the symbol for thunderstorms and either symbol for rain along the East Coast from Maine to Virginia.

Page 105
Answers will vary.

Page 106
1. F, 2. T, 3. T, 4. T, 5. F, 6. F, 7. T

Page 107
1. It should appear white., 2. It should look orange., 3. It should appear blue., 4. the flashlight light; the flashlight light. End: Since there is no air, there are no dust particles or water droplets in the sky. There are no particles to scatter the sunlight in different directions.

Page 108
1. Perseids and Geminids, 2. Ursids, 3. October 21, 4. 15 per hour, 5. Predictions can be made because the meteors are in orbit.

Page 109
Year next seen, from top: 4811; 2037; 2356; 2642; 4861; 421,969; 3649; 76,973, 1. Olber's Comet, 2. Olber's Comet; 2037, 3. Comet Tago-Sato-Kosaka; 420,000 years, 4. Answers will vary.

Page 110
Students should have 8 drawings: first all shaded, then shaded except for a crescent on the right of the Moon, next half shaded, then a shaded crescent on the left of the Moon, then no shading, then a shaded crescent on the right of the Moon, then right half shaded, and finally all shaded except for a crescent on the left of the Moon.

Page 111
1. Answers will vary., 2. 400,000 km or about 250,000 miles

Page 112
1. the planets' distances from the Sun, 2. the lengths of their years, 3. The length of the year increases with distance., 4. Pluto, 5. 4,500 million km, 6. about 30 Earth years

Page 113
Chart, from top: 1.40 kg, 4.25 kg, 1.90 kg, 13 kg, 6 kg, 5.50 kg, 7 kg, 1. Mercury, 2. Jupiter, 3. Jupiter, Saturn, Uranus, Neptune, 4. Mercury, Venus, Mars, 5. The planets are different sizes. Some have more mass than others and more gravitational pull.

Page 114
1. Moon, 2. comet, 3. meteor, 4. meteor, 5. comet, 6. Moon, comet, meteor, 7. Moon, 8. Moon, comet, 9. Moon, comet, meteor, 10. meteor, 11. meteor, 12. Moon, 13. comet

Page 115
1. A solar eclipse is a time when most of the Sun is hidden by the Moon, 2. The Moon moves between the Earth and the Sun, blocking the sunlight., 3. 7 minutes and 40 seconds

Page 116
1. During a solar eclipse, the Moon passes directly between the Sun and the Earth. Students should show the small area on the Earth where the Moon's shadow falls. A solar eclipse would be visible only from the area where the Moon's shadow falls on the Earth., 2. During a lunar eclipse, the Earth passes between the Moon and the Sun. Students should show a shadow of the Earth cast on the Moon so that the Moon cannot reflect the Sun's light. A lunar eclipse would be visible anywhere on the Earth where it is night.

Pages 123–124
1. biosphere, 2. living, 3. nonliving, (4–6 are interchangeable), 4. water, 5. food, 6. energy, 7. reproduce, 8. producers, 9. consumers, 10. decomposers, 11. herbivores, 12. carnivores, 13. omnivores, 14. populations, 15. depend, 16. environment; 17.–24. Answers may vary slightly. 17. A food pyramid gives you the amount of each type of food you need to eat to have a balanced diet., 18. It is important to know just what you are putting into your body. It helps you make good choices., 19. Some people do not want to harm animals to get food. Others want to lower their intake of fat., 20. brush, floss, and go to the dentist regularly, 21. Exercise makes muscles bigger and stronger., 22. Dangerous plants such as poison ivy, poison oak, and poison sumac can cause rashes and discomfort. Other plants such as foxglove and the Pacific yew can cause death if consumed., 23. A cut should be washed and then covered with a clean bandage., 24. Trash that may be expensive to dispose of properly may be dumped into the oceans to avoid costs. Beaches become polluted when factories dump their wastes into them. These things wash up on shore. Oil spills can pollute beaches as well.

Page 125
Living: duck, moss, ant; Nonliving: robot, orange juice, rock, cut flower, pencil., 1. Reproduction, growth and change, need for food and water, and need for energy., 2. Yes. A fungus is a form of life., 3. Answers will vary, but there is a strong likelihood that life elsewhere would reproduce, need energy, grow and develop, and need food. The details would probably be very different.

Page 126
Students' drawings should include the ocean, Earth's crust, the atmosphere, and the Sun (or sunshine). They may include plants and animals., 1. There would be no oxygen; plants and animals would die., 2. sunlight, air, minerals in rocks and soil, 3. a. insects, bacteria, plants, b. fish, whales, seals, c. birds, insects

Page 127
1. plant, grass, cricket, 2. pebbles, soil, water, 3. Answers will vary., 4. sunlight, food, and water, 5. lack of any of the things in #4

Page 128
1. The bear's fur would make it too hot in the desert., 2. The gills of the fish wouldn't help it breathe on land., 3. The legs of the moose help it walk and run in the forest. Although moose are very good swimmers, they could not live in the ocean.

Page 129
Students' answers may vary slightly. 1. Answers will vary., 2. They began to germinate., 3. the soil, the soil, 4. The seeds would not have grown; the worms may not have survived. Both need the soil to survive., 5. Answers will vary.

Page 130
Experiment should show that the newspaper squares blended with the newspaper and were not picked up as often; thus, they were "protected."

Page 131
1. flies, wings, 2. walks, legs,
3. swims and walks, flippers,
4. swims, fins and tail, 5. flies,
wings, 6. walks, legs

Page 132
1. to reach warmer areas, to find
new food sources, to raise their
young, 2. a. bighorn sheep,
b. whale, c. monarch butterfly,
d. warbler, 3. Answers will vary.

Page 133
1. true, 2. false, 3. true, 4. true,
5. true

Page 134
1. for a more accurate count,
2. Ants would have moved around
and may even have left the area.

Page 135
Answers will vary.

Page 136
Answers will vary.

Page 137
1. It has increased dramatically—
from about 1 billion to 5 billion
people. 2. The class size would
increase by about 20. The class
would probably become
overcrowded., 3. The deer
population will increase at first
because of the decrease in the fox
population. However, the deer will
exhaust the plant population. This
will result in less food for the
deer. The deer population will
then decrease.

Page 138
1. B, 2. Population B had more
food available; they are different
populations.

Page 139
1. desert, forest, marsh, 2. Student
examples will vary.; Students'
pictures will vary.

Page 140
1. cattails, water plants, algae,
reeds, grass, 2. Producers are
tomato, weed, potato, grass, and
algae., 3. The plant stores food in
its leaves, stem, and roots.

Pages 141–142
1. Photosynthesis is the process
by which plants make their own
food., 2. Chloroplasts are the
structures within the leaves that
contain the pigment chlorophyll.,
3. a. The Sun shines on the plant.,
b. The plant takes in carbon
dioxide from the air., c. Water
enters the plant., d. The
chlorophyll in the plant allows the
plant to make sugar., e. Oxygen is
released into the air., 4. nutrients,
5. water or sunlight, 6. water or
sunlight, 7. experiments,
8. Farmers

Page 143
1. a. cattle, deer, squirrels, mice,
b. foxes, coyotes, wolves, lions,
c. humans, bears, chickens,
turtles, 2. herbivore: squirrel,
carnivore: fox, omnivore: bear,
3. top: fox, hawk, robin; middle:
chipmunk, grasshopper; bottom:
nuts, berries, grass

Page 144
1. molds, yeast, and bacteria,
2. Another animal could eat it;
bacteria will break it down.,
3. Diagrams will vary. Check for
accuracy.

Page 145
Students' answers may vary
slightly. The banana slice in the
bag without the yeast does not
change as quickly. The banana
slice in the bag with the yeast is
turning brown and getting smaller.
This means that the yeast is
breaking down the banana, or
decomposing it.

Page 146
1. producer, 2. cattails, 3. water
lily, 4. starch and sugar,
5. consumer, 6. herbivore,
7. carnivore, 8. omnivore,
9. decay, 10. decomposer

Page 147
1. a. leaf>insect>bird,
b. nuts>chipmunk>hawk,
c. leaf>mouse>snake,
2. decomposers; Community
charts should show plants at
bottom., 3. sunlight>green
plant>animal>girl

Page 148
1. They increase., 2. They
decrease., 3. When there are fewer
hares for the lynx to eat, there are
fewer lynx., 4. The hare
population would decrease. There
would not be enough hares for the
lynx to eat, so the lynx population
would decrease., 5. The hare
population would get out of
control., 6. Yes. The predators and
the prey keep each population the
correct size for a balance in
nature.

Page 149
1. If the wolves and puma were
killed off, the deer would multiply
and eat all of the grasses and
leaves., 2. No. The wolves and
puma keep the deer population
balanced., 3. The insect
population would grow very large.
The insects would eat all of the
plants., 4. Predators are helpful to
keep a community in balance.

Page 150
Check graphs.; 1. during the
year when the rabbit population
was highest (1923), 2. The plant
population decreased., 3. The
rabbit population decreased.,
4. The competition for food seems
to regulate the rabbit population.

Page 151
Answers will vary. Humans are
considered omnivorous.

Page 152
1. Food webs should reflect the
following: Bottom: grass, beans,
corn, wheat, radishes. Middle:
chickens, cattle, rabbits. Top:
foxes, humans, hawks. Arrows
from grass to chickens and cattle.
Arrow from beans to rabbits.
Arrows from corn to chickens and
cattle. Arrows from grass and
wheat to cattle. Arrow from
radishes to rabbits. Arrows from
chickens to foxes, humans, and
hawks. Arrow from cattle to
humans. Arrows from rabbits to
foxes, humans, and hawks.
Decomposers on right side.,
2. Humans have polluted the
water of this stream., 3. Humans
cannot get fish from this stream.
Other animals that eat the fish
will also be affected.

Page 153
1. It was probably soft and light.,
2. Oil makes the feather heavy
and dirty., 3. The cleaning should
help the feather to get lighter.,
4. Answers will vary.

Page 154
1. The candle flame produced
more smoke., 2. a black deposit of
soot (carbon), 3. The air would be
smoky and polluted.

Page 155
1. in most cases, the square from
the outside windowsill, 2. the
square from the drawer, 3. Yes.
Students should explain that tiny
particles from many sources are
light enough to be carried through
the air., 4. Answers will vary.

Page 156
Across: 1. carbon dioxide, 5. coal,
7. eyes, 9. sunlight, 10. gases,
Down: 2. air pollution, 3. exhaust,
4. filters, 6. death, 8. lungs

Page 158
1. generally from ocean dumping
that washes back onshore,
2. bacteria, hypodermic needles,
and other medical wastes,
3. Plastic bags choke dolphins,
and plastic rings strangle diving
birds.

Page 159
Answers will vary.

Page 160
Answers will vary.

Page 161
Answers will vary.

Page 163
1. A person who eats no meat;
some vegetarians don't eat milk or
egg products either., 2. A
vegetarian diet is usually much
lower in fat. High-fat diets are a
health risk., 3. bread or cereal:
6–11; vegetables: 3–5; fruit: 2–4,
4. Answers will vary.

Page 164
1. F, 2. F, 3. T, 4. T,
5. T, 6. F, 7. T, 8. T,
9. T, 10. F, 11. brush, floss, and
visit the dentist regularly,
12. Answers will vary: forms of
exercise., 13. Healthy muscles
will support your bones better and
give you healthier, stronger joints.

Page 165
Answers will vary.

Page 167
1. Tell others where you are
going, follow a path, wear sturdy
shoes and proper clothing, and
take a container of water., 2. For a
sudden change in the weather,
take along extra layers of clothes,
a poncho, and extra snacks. For
early nightfall, plan a short trip.,
3. disease-carrying ticks and
insects; poisonous plants,
4. Answers will vary

Page 168
1. alcohol, 2. weight, 3. fat,
4. breakfast, 5. healthy, 6. sleep,
7. exercise; Secret Word: lifestyle

Page 170
Across: 2. first aid, 5. water,
6. bruise, 9. tightly, 10. pain,
11. doctor,
Down: 1. bandage, 3. injury,
4. ice, 6. blister, 7. soap, 8. burns

Page 172
1. When its oil touches the skin, it
can cause an itchy rash.,
2. Responses will vary. Accept
any response (both in and out of
the reading) that students can
verify., 3. They are both
poisonous plants that are used as
medicines., 4. to know if any
could be eaten or should never be
eaten; to know if any can cause
skin irritation or other harmful
effects